*This book is dedicated to my precious wife, Nancy,
whose prayers and love and sacrifices have made
the last forty-one years an exciting adventure.*

"Learn from the pro. Whether your view of missions is from home plate or out on the field, Tom Telford is your friend. He knows and loves churches and missions, and this book brings out the best in both."—*Leith Anderson, pastor of Wooddale Church, Eden Prairie, Minnesota*

"This book comes from the heart of Tom Telford. He has an understanding of the church in North America, a vision for world missions, and a perspective on how these two blend together. His practicality and no-holds-barred approach make this book 'must' reading for church leaders, missions committee members, missions executives, and cross-cultural missionaries."—*Paul Borthwick, missions pastor at Grace Chapel, Lexington, Massachusetts*

"When Tom explains missions to you in a classroom or church, you come to expect passion, humor, and excitement. The missions bus he drives now careens throughout the world at high speed. This book will tell you why. Enjoy the ride.—*Harvie M. Conn, professor of missions at Westminster Theological Seminary, Philadelphia, Pennsylvania*

"Missions and baseball may seem an unlikely combination, but Tom Telford scores a home run in bringing his two passions together. Drawing upon his own background as the son of a pastor-evangelist and a church missions chairman, Tom continues to learn from churches while helping them. His understanding of how to bring life and energy to missions in the local church has become legendary.

This book is glued together with personal stories of baseball and people. The reading is so enjoyable you may not realize until the end that you have experienced an education in missions."—*David Mays, Great Lakes Regional Director of ACMC*

TOM TELFORD
with Lois Shaw

MISSIONS IN THE 21ST CENTURY

Getting Your Church into the Game

Harold Shaw Publishers
Wheaton, Illinois

All Scripture quotations, unless indicated, are taken from the HOLY BIBLE, NEW INTERNATIONAL VERSION. Copyright © 1973, 1978, 1984 by the International Bible Society. Used by permission of Zondervan Publishing House. All rights reserved.

The "NIV" and "New International Version" trademarks are registered in the United States Patent and Trademark Office by the International Bible Society. Use of either trademark requires permission of the International Bible Society.

ISBN 0-87788-578-8

Edited by Mary Horner Collins and Miriam Mindeman

Cover and inside design by David LaPlaca

Library of Congress Cataloging-in-Publication Data

Telford, Tom, 1936-
    Missions in the 21st century : getting your church into the game / Tom Telford, with Lois Shaw.
      p. cm.
    Includes bibliographical references.
    ISBN 0-87788-578-8
    1. Missions. 2. Evangelistic work. 3. Twenty-first century. I. Shaw, Lois.
II. Title. III. Title: Missions in the twenty-first century.
BV3793.T45 1998
266—DC21   97-44697
                                                CIP

03   02   01   00   99   98
10 9 8 7 6 5 4 3 2

Contents

Foreword

The Old Testament records that Samson once caught three hundred foxes, tied them tail to tail in pairs, fastened burning torches to their tails, and let them loose in the standing grain of the Philistines. Tom Telford has been doing something similar: lighting fires of missionary vision and passion in churches and colleges all across America.

Samson wasn't a farmer and Tom Telford is not a missionary. He's an umpire who believes that a lot of churches are out at the plate. They are not scoring runs in world evangelization. They are playing pepper behind home plate, hitting fungoes to the outfield, and taking turns in the batting cage, but they're not really playing the game.

As a former sportswriter, I like Tom's approach to world missions because he has an umpire's candor and doesn't waffle. He tells stories from the sports world and from his own umpiring career that lend a refreshing new light on the church and missions. Perhaps this will get Christians as excited about world missions as some of them are about sports.

Looking at world missions from this perspective, Tom makes some hard calls about things churches should do to take the good news of Jesus to a lost world. Some of his rulings won't bring cheers from the grandstand, but they will force people to think about some of their cherished traditions.

On the other hand, he is not content to make judgment calls. Tom's zeal for better missionary programs shines through with a host of ideas that can be used by every church in the country, large or small. He has visited these churches and counseled them in their missions programs. He offers enough ideas for improvement to take up a year's worth of missions committee meetings.

With passion and ardor, Tom reminds Christians that the stakes are too high to quit. He appeals to them to get up and start again. Jesus is Lord of the church and he wants his people to succeed in advancing the gospel. Tom's umpiring approach to world missions will grip readers with his excitement for success.

Thousands who have heard Tom speak will thank God he has pulled his ideas together in book form. Those who haven't heard him in person are in for an exciting read. He offers the church a new kind of adventure in expanding world missions from the hobby of a few enthusiasts to the commitment of the whole church.

James Reapsome
Editor-at-large for *Evangelical Missions Quarterly* and *World Pulse Newsletter*
Wheaton, Illinois

Preface

The year after Babe Ruth retired, Tom Telford arrived.

On a July afternoon in 1936, when the New York Giants were losing their first game of a double-header, dropping them eleven games behind the front-running Chicago Cubs, Andrew and May Telford's fourth child, Tom, was born.

In the second game of the double-header that same day, New York first baseman and manager Bill Terry ignored a badly crippled knee and the orders of the Giants' team doctor, inserted himself into the lineup, and whacked a single, a double, and a triple to lead the team to victory. Terry's heroics ignited the team. They shifted into high gear and finally won the World Series that year.

Like Bill Terry, when it comes to world missions, Tom Telford has ignored some of the circumstances that might have kept another player out of the game. Telford inserts himself into the lineup and helps church missions teams win. His background as a baseball umpire gives him a unique angle on the whole missions game. It is a privilege to have a part in making available Tom's creative analysis of missions.

This book began as my master's thesis to document Tom's remarkable life and contribution to the current missions scene. It was originally written in an interview format, so the editors have left in some of the major interview questions to guide the discussion and let Tom's voice shine through. I pray that our efforts will motivate more churches to get involved in the task of sharing Christ with a needy world.

Lois Shaw
Nairobi, Kenya

Introduction

Why an Umpire Left Baseball for Missions

"Missionaries were heroes and honored guests in our house. My parents prayed for all our missionaries and their children by name in front of us kids. Missions is best caught, not taught."

How did a young boy from Philadelphia who loved baseball grow up to become enthralled with world missions?

I have the best job in the world right now. Training and motivating people to get involved in the awesome task of world missions is a privilege and honor. I love it. But the road I traveled to this point was a bit bumpy and full of miracles of God's grace.

I was born in Ottawa, Canada in 1936, the youngest of four children. My father was a pastor, and when I was about seven years old, we moved to Germantown, Pennsylvania, a town in north Philadelphia, where my father had accepted the pastorate of Berachah Church. Every summer as far back as I can remember, my father would speak at Bible conferences and we all went along as part of our summer vacation. I would check out the female population and then see what other like-minded speakers' kids were there. Percy Crawford, William Culbertson, Jack Wyrtzen, and other names come to mind.

We kids raised havoc. Sometimes when everyone else was in the meetings, we would steal the car keys from our parents and go for joy rides. One time we made holes in the walls of the conference hall and shot BB gun pellets at each other through the building. My older brother, Paul, and I were very creative when it came to trouble. One of my Sunday school teachers once told me, "Tom, if your father had been a strict disciplinarian, you'd be dead." He was probably right.

I continued to be a troublemaker and was thrown out of four schools. My parents had sacrificed much to send me to Germantown Academy in Philadelphia, and I was suspended from there twice. Once, my brother and I hitched our car up to the metal fire escape outside one of my schools and drove off, pulling the whole thing down behind us. You can imagine the uproar that caused. Not surprisingly, I became a high school dropout in tenth grade. I know that was one of many times that I broke my parents' hearts.

I'll never forget the North Mountain Bible Conference in Rickets Glenn, Pennsylvania. We were leaving after a week of meetings, and the director came out to the car and asked my father for his honorarium back. I had caused so much damage, he said, that they needed the honorarium to cover the costs.

Another reason I remember that conference was Nancy Stumpp. There was this tradition at Bible conferences of autographing each others' Bibles. I asked Nancy to sign mine and she did because, after all, I was the speaker's son. We were kids then, but we continued to see each other at camps and conferences for the next few years. I would go with my Dad to her church whenever he spoke there. We wrote once in awhile, and when I could drive, I began going to Nancy's rural church often. I saw there a very caring group of people and it created a spiritual hunger in me for that kind of fellowship.

We were married in Primrose Union Sunday School Chapel in Minersville, Pennsylvania on May 26, 1956. The place held about 75 people and I think about 150 came. I weighed 92 pounds. I know Nancy thought she was getting a gem when she married me. Instead, she got a spoiled, undisciplined, disorganized kid who was giving his life to the Lord on the installment plan. I really needed to grow up. I was restless and rebellious. In our first four years of marriage, I had seven different jobs.

You know how people talk about tough love? Nancy loved me back then with tough love. I remember one night, soon after we were married, Nancy turned out the bedroom light and said, "Tom, you carry that big Bible of yours to church and pray and sound so spiritual, but you never read it at home and you never pray with me. Why?"

Well, I did what any red-blooded American male would do—rolled over and went to sleep. It's hard to discuss things with a woman when she's right. Nancy helps bring order in the chaos in my life. We've passed the forty-year mark in our marriage, and she has stuck with me through thick and thin.

> *I know Nancy thought she was getting a gem when she married me. Instead, she got a spoiled, undisciplined, kid who was giving his life to the Lord on the installment plan.*

What were your first baseball memories, and how did you get into umpiring?

In our family we were not allowed to play sports on Sundays.

We were to do quiet things in our rooms. But we didn't live far from the old Connie Mack Stadium, and I would slip out the window to see baseball games there. In the 1940s it was a boy's dream: ten cents for bus fare, seventy-five cents for a seat in the bleachers, five cents for peanuts. If there wasn't a game at the stadium, we'd often play sandlot baseball.

As an adult, I was much more interested in the major leagues than world missions. I played for our church softball team and became its manager. Baseball became a constant in my life. I went to clinics and eventually began umpiring locally.

> *You have to be a tough, scrappy person to be a good umpire— maybe all pastors should go to umpire school.*

Some of the scouts that watched me umpire invited me to the Major Leagues Umpire Development Program for six weeks. It was a tough program. We studied and trained from morning until night. There were hundreds of rules and we had to learn them all, inside out. We were divided into groups and they would give us a test with one hundred questions. We had to get them all right. If everyone on the team got them all, they'd give you a keg of beer. I didn't care about the keg of beer, but watch out if you were the guy that let your team down with one or two wrong.

It was intense. You have to be a tough, scrappy person to be a good umpire. You have to be able to handle people yelling at you in tight situations and not lose it. You have to be willing to have 50 percent of the people believe you are wrong 50 percent of the time. You know, maybe all pastors should go to umpire school!

I was offered an umpiring position in the minor leagues.

But by God's grace I was able to see that it was no life for a Christian with a family. You are constantly on the road, staying away for long stretches without seeing your wife. Frankly, it's a tough crowd.

Instead, in 1970 I started the Telford Officials Association, an umpire training school that ultimately trained over 140 umpires while it was open. We provided umpires for high schools and colleges all around the greater Philadelphia area and some of my umpires went on to the minor leagues.

What would you say was the highlight of your baseball career?

Without question, the highlight of my career was when I was asked to umpire for the National League when the major league umpires went on an illegal strike in 1972.

Ruly Carpenter, the owner of the Philadelphia Phillies, called and asked the Telford Officials Association to provide the umpiring lineup for the games. I can still feel the thrill of being on the field, talking and joking with players like Mike Schmidt, Dave Winfield, and Pete Rose, people I'd never dreamed of meeting. Every game was on television, so we were afraid to make any mistakes. I remember when the officials would get back to the dressing room, we would all congratulate each other, "We pulled it off! We didn't blow any calls!"

In bad weather, it's the umpire's job to call the game or decide on a rain delay. Once I had to make the rain delay decision with thousands of fans and players waiting for the verdict. Another time, I threw Tommy Lasorda, the manager of the L. A. Dodgers, out of a game for disputing a call. Pete Rose, who was with the Phillies at that time, would joke around and call me "bus driver." (That's what I did for a second job.) The media was everywhere. There were articles

in the newspaper every day for or against us. I was inter-
viewed on television. I have letters at home from owners and
managers. It was an amazing experience.

Umpiring in the major leagues was a once in a lifetime
opportunity. As Casey Stengel says, "There comes a time in
every man's life and I've had a lot of them." I'm grateful for
those thrilling times, but I love what I'm doing now so much
more than all of that.

What brought about your career move from umping for baseball to stumping for missions?

To answer that I have to go back to the people God placed
in my life. In the early 1960s, I had been serving as the
missions chairman at my church. I went at the job like an
umpire would. I wanted to know the rules of the game, what
worked and what didn't. I was always
asking questions and trying to figure
out what would make missions work
better in our church. You know what
umpires say, "When you walk on the
field, you're god." I like that take-
charge feeling and knowing what
I'm doing. So I thought I was running a pretty good missions program at our church.

> *I went at the job of missions chairman like an umpire would. I wanted to know the rules of the game, what worked and what didn't.*

Our pastor, Donald Hubbard,
told me about ACMC (Advancing
Churches in Missions Commitment), an organization that offered
national conferences to train and
motivate local church missions committee members. He suggested I go
to the next conference. Secretly I thought, *What can they teach*

me? I'm doing a great job. I could probably teach them *a thing or two.* I was so arrogant and had such an attitude. But God had a little plan up his sleeve. When I got to the meetings, I was completely blown away. I didn't miss one meeting at that conference and I have never missed an ACMC conference since. That was 1972, and it was a turning point in my life.

Another pastor, Ron Miller, used to say, "Tom, you have missions written all over you!" He would often challenge me to consider getting more involved somehow. About that time I met Eugene Williams, then the head of American Missionary Fellowship. He offered me a job as a regional director for AMF, which scared me half to death. I didn't want to tell Nancy. I figured she'd want me to do it. We discussed it and ultimately decided against it. But that offer really made me think.

The year following the ACMC conference, I was consumed with missions in the local church. I came back from the conference with 101 new ideas to change things in our church and I came in like gangbusters. As you know, that's not the way things work in most churches. A lot of churches have an unspoken motto that says, "We never did it that way before." Anyway, I almost lost my shirt because of my enthusiasm. Once again my umpire training helped me because I was able to talk my way through some tough committee meetings.

In 1977 I was elected to the ACMC board. Four years later, Carl Palmer and John Bennett asked me to work with the organization full time. I said no and I had a dozen reasons why. I sounded like Moses: "I'm scared to death to speak publicly. I don't even have a high-school education. So I can't do this job because the job description says you have to be a seminary graduate."

Another excuse I had was my age. I was too old for this, and the idea of raising my own support scared me. But a friend, Tom Kenney, took me out for coffee one day. He knew I was struggling about beginning a second career in ministry at my age and told me how his dad had started working with the student ministry of InterVarsity Christian Fellowship about the time most men were retiring. As Tom described what God had done in his dad's life, I was so encouraged. I don't think he ever knew what that time over a cup of coffee did for me.

I'm not sure how the board got around the other requirements, but they broke all the rules to hire me. In 1982 I began working full time with ACMC. I had so much to learn. But God has surrounded me with smart folks who share with me what they know.

Can you tell us about some of the role models who have influenced your life?

My father was my first role model. Even in my rebellious years, I could never deny that Christ was everything to my father and mother. People tell me I'm single-minded and I know I saw that in my dad.

My father graduated from Moody Bible Institute. He just showed up one day at Moody with his luggage and said, "I'm here to study to be a pastor." They explained to him that it's not done like that; you have to apply and be accepted. But somehow he stayed and eventually graduated. He even spent some time in Argentina as a missionary. He had one passion and that was preaching the gospel. He preached well into his nineties.

When we moved to the church in Philadelphia, my father came without the promise of any salary. When I think of that today, it seems crazy. But you know, God blessed him for that, and it's a model of faith I still think about. The church didn't even take up an offering. They had a box on the wall at the back, and whatever people put in that box went to our salary and missions. From day one, my father said that 50 percent of everything that was given went to world missions.

Missionaries were heroes and honored guests in our house. We saved the best of what we had for missionaries. My parents prayed faithfully for all our missionaries in front of us kids. We knew the missionaries' names, the names of their children, where they lived, and what they did. I realize now what a powerful impact that had on me. I always say that missions is best caught, not taught.

My wife, Nancy, has been a support and role model for me. It was through watching her study God's Word and pray in our early married life that I slowly came around. I'm convinced that we can teach so much by what we do and what we model. If we pray, if we trust, others will be encouraged to do the same. One time my grandson was going upstairs to bed and called, "Grandpa, I'm going up to say my prayers. Do you need anything from God?" We need to watch what we do because people are copying us.

> *Missions is best caught, not taught.*

I worked with ACMC for fifteen years and met many people who have become my role models, mentors, and teachers. Carl Palmer, pastor of Cedar Mill Bible in Portland, Woody Phillips, director of United World Mission, Gordon MacDonald from Grace Chapel near Boston—these guys have taught me things about missions and the local church that I never dreamed possible. I have friends like Charlie Quarles, retired from Du Pont after a successful career, who wanted to get involved in missions somehow. You know what he does for me? All the things I'm terrible at doing. He organizes my conferences and puts my letters and schedules on the computer. Nothing is too small a job for Charlie. He models Christ to me.

These role models and friends are God's miracles of grace in my life and are the reason I left baseball for missions. No question about that call. Motivating churches to get involved in spreading the gospel and supporting missionaries is the thing I love doing most. I often say, "People are not good at listening, but are great at imitating." And I guess my single focus shows, even to kids. One time I had been away from my home church for quite a few weeks speaking at conferences and seminars. The Sunday I was back in church, a little girl sitting behind me whispered rather loudly to her mother, "Mommy, Mr. Missions just came in!" I can live with that.

Rooting for the Home Team

If you ask any baseball fan over forty years of age what is missing from the game today, chances are they will say "loyalty." Take me, for instance. I am a Chicago Cubs fan. This means that I have to endure a certain stigma: *loser*. But no matter what, they are my home team.

I fell in love with the Cubs while I was a student in college in the Chicago area. I used to cut class and head down to Wrigley Field to watch them play. I meet people who say, "I'm a Phillies fan. I started following them when they won the World Series" or "I'm an Atlanta Braves fan. I began following them when they beat the Indians in the World Series." I began following the Cubs in 1975 when they finished in last place, seventeen games out of first place. (You would have to be over sixty years old to have become a Cubs fan when they went to the World Series.)

To be a Cubs fan means you have to look at events from a certain perspective. The impact of the recent news that one of the American League teams (the Milwaukee Brewers) would move to the National League was met with disdain by some who shrieked for "the purity of the game." To us Cub fans it meant that now maybe we had the chance to finish in *sixth* place instead of fifth.

Maybe it is the daytime baseball, the fresh grass and bright green ivy on the centerfield wall. Maybe it is the red, white and blue uniforms that link them with Americana. It may even be the single superstar wallowing in a swamp of mediocrity. . . . I don't know. All I know is that the Cubs can't afford to lose me.

—Rick Mead, *Director of Vietnamese/Filipino Ministry with International Teams, Philadelphia*

1
The Home Team

Common Missions Errors Local Churches Should Avoid

"The church shouldn't call for volunteers; it should set up a draft."

The task of world missions is a team effort between local churches, mission agencies, and individuals who are called by God. People don't become missionaries just because they think it might be a good idea after hearing a dynamic speaker at a missions conference. The old hymn says "whosoever will may come," not necessarily "whosoever will may *go*." The local church must be behind missionaries all the way.

I wholeheartedly agree with Michael Griffiths' statement in his book *Get Your Church Involved in Missions:* "The most that an individual can do is express his [or her] *willingness*. Others must determine his *worthiness*. The individual may be free to go, but only his church knows if he is really fitted to go." The local church is the starting place.

What role should the local church play in the arena of world missions?

Part of the reason there's such a fierce loyalty to baseball today is due to having a home team. That's the group of guys you love, hate, and cry over. When your team wins, you cheer; when they lose, you suffer. The home team solicits and generates the interest and love for the game.

> *The home church is where missionaries are chosen, cheered on, and supported.*

The local church has a similar role as the "home team" in the game of missions. It's where enthusiasm and loyalty to world evangelization is generated. It's where missionaries are chosen, cheered on, and supported.

But I do have some concerns about churches today. It's not easy being the home team. I've observed a few common "errors" that many churches make as they relate to mission agencies and missionaries. I mention these not as judgments, but as suggestions for making church teams stronger.

Error #1: No Draft

Church growth specialist C. Peter Wagner says that possibly only one percent of all American evangelicals have the missionary gift. I believe it is the local church's responsibility to discern and discover who in the congregation has that gift. My first concern is that many churches fail to watch for members with missionary potential and challenge them to missionary service. They do not take a proactive role in selecting and screening missionary candidates. The church shouldn't call for volunteers, but set up a draft.

When the church is investing thousands of the Lord's dollars into a ministry, they have the right to recruit. In this way, churches and missionary agencies can really work together. If a church has prayed about and recruited an individual who is called of God, then it's hard for an agency to say no. Any mission agency worth its salt must have the recommendation and endorsement of the missionary's local church. And it works the other way too. The discerning church can also say no to someone they believe is not ready. This decision may then be confirmed by the mission agency program a candidate goes through.

Error #2: No relationship with mission agencies

Churches often fail to build relationships of mutual trust and understanding with mission agencies they support. I often compare it to sending your own child overseas, say, for a student exchange program. Would you pay $50,000 to a group to send your child overseas and not know anything about the organization? Wouldn't you want to know the director of the organization and how the organization functions? I hope so.

Similarly, churches who are recruiting missionaries have the responsibility to do a thorough study of the agencies they will serve with. When I first became a missions chairman, I knew next to nothing about the agencies our church supported. So I took my two-week vacation, and Nancy and I got in our old car and visited every agency our church was involved with. I introduced myself: "I'm from so and so church and we have some missionaries out under your mission. Could someone spend a little time with me and tell me about your operation here? What do you do with the money we send you? What are your objectives? Do you feel you are succeeding?"

A couple of the mission agencies wouldn't let me past the

front door. One didn't have anyone who could answer my questions right then. Another told me they didn't have the time and could I please put my questions in a letter? We were giving thousands of dollars a year to this one agency and they said they didn't have the time to answer my questions. Needless to say, I felt confused. Our church was giving these agencies large chunks of money through our missionaries, and they didn't seem to think it was any of our business to know about them.

> *If you're giving your sons and daughters and your money to a mission agency, you'd better find out all you can about it.*

If you're giving your sons and daughters and your money to an agency, you'd better find out all you can about it. Make sure they know you. There's just no short cut to that. The church needs to take initiative with this. I suggest that you build good relationships with a few good agencies. Find five or six agencies with which your people feel comfortable and your church mission statement is compatible and stay with them.

Error #3: Church leaders don't take responsibility

The church of Christ was entrusted with the responsibility of world evangelization, wasn't it? It's our mandate and our top priority. In many cases though, church leaders fail to take adequate responsibility for the work their missionary is sent to do and also for the spiritual welfare of the missionary. I know this puts a lot of responsibility on the shoulders of church leaders, but I believe it's the right thing to do.

I visit more than 100 churches every year and have many varied experiences with missions committees and church leaders. On one visit recently, I saw what a difference it makes, for the missionary and the church, when the church gets involved in these areas.

This particular church was having a missions prayer meeting before the committee meeting, so I joined in. They were talking about a single missionary woman who had come home to bury her mother. She was an only child and it had been a difficult time. She was back on the field and the church was getting news that she was having a hard time. The pastor got up and said, "I was talking to our missionary on the phone this week and she is really suffering. I think we ought to pray for her for the next half hour." So we prayed. Then a young woman stood up and said, "I'm her best friend. What if I just went and lived with her for a few weeks? I have some personal leave I can take from work."

They discussed the costs and the airfare, and prayed about it. They decided to put the offering plates at the back that night and see if they could help raise the money. Well, before the evening was over, they had raised the money to send this woman to be with her friend! That's what I mean by taking responsibility for your missionary.

Churches sometimes send their pastors to counsel and encourage missionaries, or provide the means for them to have counseling when they come home. If a missionary has a major financial concern or medical need, the sending church needs to find out what they can do to help. Be aggressive and contact the agency. Don't wait to hear about the need when it's all over and done.

Error #4: Corporate denial

Just like some missionary organizations, churches often assume a "rose-colored glasses" attitude which denies missionary incompetence. They don't want to face changes which indicate the need for a person's reassignment or even dismissal. Someone may ask, "You mean fire a missionary?" Possibly.

I've learned a lot of things the hard way. For many years I was so enthusiastic about missions, I assumed all missionaries were doing a great job and could handle whatever came along. I never considered the reality of severe problems or incompetence in missionaries. However, in one church where I served, it became clear that a family we supported needed to be brought home for help. The couple was having marital problems and their work had come to a complete standstill. As the missions chairman, the church finally flew me over to meet with them.

> *We often assume a "rose-colored glasses" attitude which denies missionary incompetence. Someone may ask, "You mean fire a missionary?"*

I sat down with the family and told them the church wanted to bring them home. We even offered to redeploy them in another ministry or another job. Their teenaged son tried to punch me and said, "How can you say this to my dad? Who do you think you are, God?" The parents absolutely refused to admit anything was wrong. It was very difficult. But what was more difficult was the response when I got home. The elders wouldn't follow through on my recommendation. This couple had so many friends in the congregation that they felt it would cause too many problems. So that church continued supporting ineffective missionaries for a number of years with God's money because it lacked the courage to pull them out. If they had been on staff at the church, they would have been let go—I'm sure of it.

That's why I say we often wear rose-colored glasses when

looking at our missionaries. We have a dual standard when it comes to our local church staff and our overseas personnel. It needs to be admitted and changed.

Error #5: Poor preparation of missionary candidates

Churches are not only to pray for God to raise up missionaries from their own ranks, but they also are to prepare missionary appointees for service and the adjustments before they leave. This can be done by providing opportunities for cross-cultural experience and ministry, teaching teamwork skills, and mentoring, counseling, and expecting accountability from them.

I realize that this is asking a lot of a local church. But I think it's a mistake to hand all of this responsibility over to a mission agency. What is the basic commodity the church has to offer? Isn't it people and resources? If we don't handle these properly at the local church level, we're not doing our job. Let me explain what I mean, and why this is not something an agency can always do.

A number of years ago when I was an enthusiastic young missions chairman, if any live body had come up to me in any condition and said, "I want to be a missionary," I'd have said, "You're there." And I would have done everything in my power to get that person to the field as fast as possible. In my first couple of years as chairman, I saw four couples go to the field, fully supported, in record time. I was proud of myself and our missions program. It's a competitive edge I have. But here's the sad part: two of those couples came back and never returned.

I've often wondered what contributed to these missionaries not making it overseas. One reason was that in my enthusiasm, I pushed people overseas and sometimes they went too soon. We also didn't do a good job of preparing them, mentoring them, and seeing how they could serve and use their gifts at home first.

I'll never forget my experience with one of these couples when they returned home from their first term. When I went to visit them, the woman met me at the door, crying, "We're not going back. The last four years of our life can only be described as hell!" She explained how they had worked with another couple from another mission who always seemed to have all the money they ever needed, while she and her husband had had to scrounge for everything. She talked about their many other struggles. "We can't go back, Tom," she confided, "but we're afraid to tell the church. How can we tell all these people who have supported us for four years?"

We decided that a good starting point was just to be honest, and I agreed to tell the church for them. It was one of the hardest things I have ever had to do. It didn't go well. In fact it was terrible. They were living in the missionary apartments and were very visible. They were treated as second-class Christians and failures for some time. You see, missionaries are not allowed to fail or to leave the job. The rest of us can, but not missionaries.

> **Missionaries are not allowed to fail or to leave the job. The rest of us can, but not missionaries.**

But that's not the end of the story. The couple got counseling, got back on their feet, and he became the pastor of a small church on the other side of the state. One day he called and said, "We still feel God has called us to be church planters. Could you help us?" I referred them to the American Missionary Fellowship, a group that reopens closed churches across America. And you know what? They have been with AMF for twenty years and are clearly in the right place now.

That experience made me do a lot of hard thinking about pushing people onto the mission field. Now I try to slow them down. The church must do an adequate job of giving candidates opportunities to prepare and prove themselves.

Error #6: Lack of communication about lifestyle issues

There is a real need for churches and agencies to have some general agreement on missionary lifestyle overseas and on the home office costs. This area of money is one that still needs a lot of attention.

A young couple in my church was struggling to raise an unusually high support level. They were going to an Eastern European country and most of the costs were very legitimate and necessary, but it was all a bit overwhelming. As their missions chairman, I sat down with them and we went over all the costs together. "Could you get along on a bit less in this category, or over here in this area?" I prodded. We came up with a proposal and I took it to the agency for them. The agency was willing to go with the suggestions of this couple and they were released to go overseas.

I tell you this to illustrate a couple of things. One, is that we need to have a liaison between the mission agency, the church, and the missionary. Second, when it comes to finances, we need to see one another not as adversaries but as co-workers. Sometimes we just need to talk. Finances will always be a sensitive subject, so we might as well talk about it.

Churches often place agencies in catch-22 situations. They expect more and more in support services from agencies and at the same time complain about high agency overhead costs. They oppose administrative deductions from the missionaries' support but avoid contributing to the agencies' home office needs.

The other side of the coin is that Christians often fail to develop a biblical view of materialism and don't model a kingdom lifestyle. If more churches thought through these issues, they would produce more disciplined, countercultural, self-sacrificing, nonmaterialistic, missionary candidates who are more content, able to give up their rights, willing to submit to one another, equipped to suffer hardship, and experienced at relying on God.

I have had to struggle with lifestyle issues in my own life. My dream was to move out of my row house in Philadelphia into a single-family home. I worked for twenty-two years, and finally we were able to buy our little dream home. It was just about that time that I was considering working with ACMC, who told me that I would have to go out and "discover my support." It was a very difficult time for me. We wrestled with having to sell that house and downsize so I could do this ministry. I felt God urging me to give it up. How could I? How could I ask my wife to do this? I kept saying, "No. I'm not going to give it up."

> **Churches need to demonstrate to the world a lifestyle that is free from the grip of possessions.**

Finally, one night I got so burdened and convicted about it that I got up in the middle of the night, painted a "For Sale" sign, and posted it on my front lawn at two o'clock in the morning! Later, we moved into a house one-quarter the size of what we sold.

In America we are so wrapped up in our possessions and competing with the Joneses, that we forget the important things. Churches most of all need to demonstrate to the world, and to their potential missionaries, a lifestyle that is free from the grip of possessions.

Error #7: No workable missions policy and strategy

Churches often fail to develop a workable, directive missions policy and strategy for their decision making—and then stick to it. I can hear some churches saying, "Tom, our policy is to just pray, let the Spirit guide, and handle each case as it comes up." If that's the case, then your decision making becomes like a beauty contest: This couple is nice, their kids are well-behaved, he's very articulate, so they are chosen. Is that how you hire a pastor? No. You have a solid list of criteria and requirements by which you choose the right pastor for your congregation. And the same is needed for choosing missionaries.

No church can do everything. You have to focus.

It's a very different ball game than it was twenty-five years ago. Some churches I know get hundreds of applications for missionary support every year. How in the world can churches make good decisions case-by-case with all that is involved? It is essential to have good policies in place. You can't just casually sit around in a committee room, read a request for support and say, "Well, what do you think? Should we take them on?" That shocks me, but some churches do it. We used to joke around at our missions committee meetings, saying that if the missionary had presented a couple of good slides and the Phillies had won that afternoon, we'd feel inclined to say, "Let's support them." But if the next week, the church had had a crisis and the Phillies had lost, then that poor missionary didn't have a chance!

We need some objective guidelines that reflect the church's commitments and priorities. A missions policy helps a church decide where they want to go in missions, what kinds of ministries and people they want to support, and in what parts of the world they want to focus. No church can do everything. You have to focus.

I'm not going to say this makes life easy. Let me tell you how hard it can be to have to stick to a set policy. The missions committee of our church had just forged policy guidelines for supporting missionaries. As the chairman, I had been mobilizing the young people in our church for missions by spending time with some of the key leaders of our youth. One guy, I'll call him Bob, was a high school senior, and the year I got to know him, he led about fifteen students in his school to the Lord. He was a great kid.

Bob went off to college and did four years in three. (He was also a smart guy.) While he was there, he worked in a home for kids with addiction problems. After graduating and getting married, he and his wife wanted to start a ministry with these hurting youth. So Bob wrote to our church about their plans.

Well, our missions policy stated that a certain percentage could be used for this kind of ministry, but we had already allocated those funds for a program in our area. The statement also suggested that ministries of this kind should be supported by the local churches in the area. Bob would not be working near our church. So in two respects, the church could not get involved. Although the church respected Bob and his wife, they voted not to support them.

I was devastated because I had poured so much of myself into these two. I put off telling them for three weeks because it hurt so badly. When Bob and his wife attended a missions conference at our church, I took them aside to tell them the news. Before I could say anything, Bob handed me an envelope with a note, "Dear Tom and Nancy: You have meant so much to us as a couple, and we believe so much in what you are doing with ACMC, that we saved the cash gifts from our wedding and we want you to have this for your ministry." Enclosed was a check for a large sum.

I took them into a back room because I'm an emotional guy and I knew I'd have trouble talking. I said, "I want you guys to look out the window because I can't face you. The church has decided not to support you." I had just gotten those words out of my mouth when they both put their arms around me and said, "Tom, we've read the missions policy of this church and we knew they couldn't take us on financially. We wrote the letter because we had friends here and we wanted their prayer support. Can we be in the church's listing of missionaries so you will pray for us?" That experience made a believer out of me as far as a missions policy goes.

To really enter the game of missions these days, churches must not fail to mobilize and train new missionaries from their congregations, build relationships with mission agencies, and draw up clear missions policies. Now there's an exciting home-team effort.

FAN FARE

At the World Series

One of my biggest thrills was covering the 1947
World Series between the New York Yankees and
the Brooklyn Dodgers. I was a nineteen-year-old
sportswriter in those days for the town paper in
Lancaster, Pennsylvania. I took the train to New
York City, and then the subway to Ebbets Field in
Brooklyn for game five. The Series was tied two
games each. It seemed like every game in that
Series was a nailbiter. Ebbets Field was one of those
old cozy ballparks like Forbes Field in Pittsburgh
and Connie Mack Stadium in Philadelphia. All
three have since perished at the hands of the
wrecker's ball.

Police barricades were erected all around the
stadium, so that was the first place I had to show
my press pass. This was Saturday, October 4, the
day after the fourth game in which Dodger Cookie
Lavagetto had smashed a double off the right field
wall, with two outs in the ninth inning. The Dodgers won, 3-2, and the fans poured into right field
to view the spot on the wall. Dick Young of the *New
York Daily News* wrote that they stood there "as the
lame and the halt stand at the shrine in Lourdes."

Once admitted to Ebbets Field, I went first to
claim my seat in the press box. After that I went
down to the field to interview the players. That was
worth it all. Then, probably my second biggest
thrill was the free lunch. The Series is handout time
for the press, but I had never seen such a spread.

The game itself again came down to a ninth-inning resolution, but the roles were reversed from the day before. The Yankees led, 2-1, going into the ninth as they had the day before. Once again Dodger batter Cookie Lavagetto came to the plate with two outs and the tying run at second. He took an inside fast ball for a strike, and then three straight balls. The crowd screamed. Lavagetto took a second strike. Then Spec Shea of the Yankees threw another fast ball, and Lavagetto swung and missed. The Yankees won. Sportswriter Roger Kahn wrote, "Heroism in the batter's box is a sometime thing." I was rooting for Brooklyn, but the Dodgers lost the 1947 World Series in seven games. What a Series!

—*James Reapsome, editor-at-large of* Evangelical Missions Quarterly *and* World Pulse Newsletter

2
Scouting the Minor Leagues

Why Recruitment Is Vital

"When God calls us, he usually calls loud enough that our church and friends who know us can hear it too."

Just as a baseball scout will comb the minor league teams for possible draft picks, churches need to seek out and recruit the best people they have to serve in missions. I am always looking for creative and innovative people to work on the missions committee or to consider missions as a career. But that task is not always easy.

How can the local church go about getting people into the missions game?

There was one woman in our church I thought would make an ideal committee member. She was creative, had lots of good ideas, and was a Bible college graduate. So I asked her to consider being an intern for six months and then to come on the missions committee. She looked me straight in the eye and said, "That's the last committee in the church that I would ever want to be on, and I'll give you three reasons why. One, I don't like missions. Two, I don't like you. Three, I don't like your haircut. So the answer is no!"

Well, reasons number two and three didn't bother me, but reason number one did bother me. Not liking missions? I argued with her for about ten minutes and then gave up.

About a week later my phone rang, and it was this woman. She apologized for the first reason she had given (but not the other two). She had thought about it and decided she wanted to intern and work toward being on the committee. She did what was required of her and six months later joined the missions committee. But that's not the end of the story.

A year later we got together for lunch and she told me that God was calling her to the mission field. We concurred, and she went on to serve as a teacher at Faith Academy, a school for missionary kids in the Philippines. That's what I mean by recruitment! It begins with a challenge, and God takes it from there.

Isn't it God's job to call people to volunteer for missions, and not ours?

As I look through the New Testament, Jesus did not use the volunteer system in his close circle of relationships. He chose and recruited his disciples. How did he recruit them? He prayed, initiated the relationships, and said, "Come, follow me" (see Matthew 4:18-22, Luke 5:1-11, Luke 6:12-16). I believe one of the reasons we see a high rate of failure among missionaries is because people have made decisions to go into missions without the counsel and blessing of

> *Jesus did not use the volunteer system in his close circle of relationships.*

church leaders. It is a dangerous thing to make major ministry decisions apart from the body of Christ. My pastor often says, "Don't let people lay hands on themselves." An individual must certainly feel called of God and have a willing heart. But when God calls people, he usually calls loud enough that their church and friends who know them can hear it too. As I've mentioned before, the church community must help confirm that person's call and his or her readiness for service.

I believe strongly in recruiting but, like anything, it can be done poorly. Let me give you a number of important principles I have discovered about what is involved in missions recruitment.

Recruitment requires mentoring.

Anybody who hangs around with me very long has heard me say: "We teach what we know; we reproduce what we are." Jesus spent time investing his life into the disciples' lives. He encouraged their strengths and challenged them on their weak points. Just looking at the conversations he had with Peter would make a good study in mentoring.

When I accepted the job with ACMC and knew I would be leaving my post as missions chairperson at my church, I started looking around for someone to mentor and train for that position. I knew a committed young man in our church named Dan who was a high school teacher of social studies, world government, and international studies. I saw some real strengths in him and asked him to consider joining the missions committee. Up to that point, he had not been involved in missions at all. I told him I'd give him a couple of hours a week, and asked him to go to meetings and conferences with me and generally follow me around. We would also meet periodically after his classes and knock ideas around.

With his knowledge of world events, he was ideal for a

missions chairperson. I was not the only one who felt that way. He did eventually take over my job and has done a far better job than I ever did. He knows a lot about international issues and he and his wife Sharon have put together some tremendous missions ideas. He's done things I'd never dreamed of. It was kind of humbling for me, but I'm very proud of Dan. In addition, Dan has taken both of his sabbatical years and taught overseas at Rift Valley Academy, a boarding school with over 500 missionary kids in Kenya, East Africa. He's a man of missions.

Like Jesus, a mentor also has to be willing to point out your weaknesses. When I first began working with ACMC, I was traveling and speaking a lot. One time I traveled with a man named Greg Livingstone who is now the CEO of Frontiers Mission. One evening after we had shared the pulpit, we were driving to our next engagement. For half an hour, Greg told me everything I had done wrong. I was used to people telling me how great I was and here this guy was cutting me down. If that wasn't enough, Greg also sent me a letter following up everything he had said verbally!

But you know what? The next time I got up to speak, I think I was a better man for it. I had learned some things. Mentoring is encouraging someone's strengths and helping that person through his or her weaknesses.

Recruitment requires discernment.

The local church needs to figure out what qualities are needed, then draft qualified people for the task of missions. We're not infallible here, but over time we can gain discernment and learn more about people and about what makes good missionaries.

Once I was teaching a session at Columbia International University on the qualifications for a missionary. We happened to be meeting in an auditorium that could seat about

300 people. However, there were only about twenty-five students in the class. Well, there was one guy who always sat off by himself. It bugged me. After two days of this, I called him over after class and said, "I have a question. Why on earth do you sit over there all by yourself?"

"I really don't like people," he said.

"What are you training to be?"

"I'm thinking about missions," he said.

"You're out of your mind," I responded. "Listen, I'm really tired right now. I've just been teaching for two hours, but if you don't sit with the rest of the class tomorrow, I'm going to flunk you."

That night he showed up at my office. He said his church had sent him to seminary and he was kind of a role model for the young people. "You'd better start working on your people skills or you're wasting your time," I said. "And by the way, what's the name of your church and your pastor's name?"

So I called the guy's pastor and I really lit into him for sending someone to seminary who didn't even like to be with people. Some of my old umpire training came through and, as you know, "we call them as we see them." I wasn't as gentle as I should have been. I know I'll never hear from that guy. But loving people is essential for missionaries.

> *Loving people is essential for missionaries. An umpire may get stuck with a rotten team manager, but he has to get along with him for nine innings.*

An umpire may get stuck with a rotten team manager, but he has to get along with him for nine innings. He has to make it work. If he can't adjust, then he's out of there. Once churches discern what qualities make a good missionary, then they need to find and recruit those kind of people.

Recruitment requires finding the "Joeys."

The idea here is that churches need to seek out people who want to be missionaries more than anything. Let me give you an example of what I mean.

One of my best umpire friends had a brother named Joey. Joey was an average baseball player in high school and he did very well in college. But he wasn't all that great of a player. One time I was umpiring a game Joey played in, and afterward asked him what he wanted to do after college.

"I want to be in the major leagues so bad. I don't care if I have to polish the players' shoes, I want to make it, Tom. I'll do anything."

After college he was placed in a semipro league but did not get drafted. He was brokenhearted. Well, a lot of semipro players that don't get drafted are given what they call a "six-pack": they pay a pack of guys $600, send them down to Florida for spring training and have a look at them. So Joey went to spring training camp. He really didn't have a shot at the major leagues, but the guy worked at it. He was the first one on the field every day and the last one off. He ate and slept baseball.

The end of the story? Joey became a minor league player and then went on to pitch in the major leagues for five years, and is now a pitching coach for the Boston Red Sox. The newspaper articles always described him as a guy who worked hard on the fundamentals. That's what eventually makes a good player. I will talk later about what the fundamentals are for training a missionary, but right now, my point is that churches need to recruit people who want to be involved in missions outreach so badly they can taste it. We need to find the Joeys in our churches, because they are the ones who will make it in the big leagues in missions.

Recruitment requires having to say no.

Once when the umpire Pinelli called Babe Ruth out on strikes, the Babe thought the crowd was on his side, so he said, "There are 40,000 people out there who know that last one was a ball, tomato head!" And Pinelli replied, "Maybe so, but mine's the only opinion that counts." Sometimes the church will not be on your side when you have to say no to a recruit, and that's a hard one.

A man I'll call Mike was a young seminary grad in our church who told me he wanted to be a missionary. I wasn't so sure he had the right stuff. So I called Mike's professors at seminary and they unanimously agreed, "Mike just doesn't have what it takes. He'll never be a missionary in a million years." Our pastor at that time was also hesitant, so he suggested, "Why don't we give Mike a job here at the church and see how he does?" So we gave him a single adult class and within one year the class went from forty attendees to fifteen. We gave him another job with similar results.

I called him into my office and he broke down and cried. He had spent four years preparing to be a missionary. He had married a woman who had graduated with him with the same goal. Instead of saying, "You'll *never* make a missionary," I've learned to turn it around and say, "My job is to find out where you will fit." There are lots of career tests and services that help indicate people's giftedness and capabilities. The church can make use of these to help people discern what they are good at.

It's never easy to say no, but when you're spending thousands of dollars of the Lord's money, it's an important part of recruiting.

Recruitment requires modeling.

We live in a world that's desperately looking for role models. Ask any Little League kid who he wants to play like and he'll tell you in the snap of a finger who his hero is in the major leagues. We all want to be like someone we admire. We can successfully recruit people, young and old, from our churches if we parade excellent role models in front of them.

There was an elder in our church who, at age 53, began to seriously consider missions. One night he and his wife fasted and prayed for God's guidance. That night, "by chance," some people stopped by their house when their car broke down. They were on their way to a mission agency and asked for a ride there. So they drove these people to the agency and—you guessed it—that weekend at the agency they signed on to go to Mongolia! The church warmly endorsed their call and they are now the field leaders for all the mission agencies working together in Mongolia.

> *We can successfully recruit people, young and old, from our churches if we parade excellent role models in front of them.*

What a great model they have been for others considering missions work, especially as a second career. Their example also influenced their four daughters, who are all involved in missions now as well.

Great missionary biographies that are well-written can also provide role models for your family. I know a family who once read *Bruchko,* the powerful story of Bruce Olson's missionary endeavors in South America. The children were teenagers, and many times they had to stop reading because they all were in tears. When they read the last chapter and closed the book, both children said, "I want to serve Jesus and be willing to give my life like Bruchko did." It was a spontaneous response to a role model. Good missions books can provide powerful models.

Recruitment should start at your own church.

I was in a church not long ago that boasted a missions budget of half a million dollars. They were quite pleased about it. When I got up to speak, I asked how many of their own young people had been commissioned to overseas ministry in the last ten years. There was not one. That is wrong.

On a plane ride recently, I was seated next to a well-dressed young man. As we chatted he asked me what I do for a living. I often find it hard to explain what local church missions motivation is in one sentence, so I just said, "I'm a missions specialist." His eyes lit up and he said, "You know what our denomination does in missions? Every family in the church must raise the money to send every one of their children on a missions trip at some point in their teenage years." He explained that they believed first-hand exposure was the ideal way to get young people and families turned on to missions as central to the ministry of the church. I was thrilled.

Then he told me he was Mormon.

I thought to myself, if every evangelical church in America did what the Mormons are doing, we wouldn't have two billion people going to hell! We need to be looking for and recruiting folks from our churches who want to invest their lives in world evangelization.

Recruitment requires prayer.

A few years ago my church was hosting a large ACMC conference. It was a very busy time for me because I was responsible for all the details. It was Saturday afternoon and I was exhausted. So I went into the church library just to sit down for a couple of minutes and close my eyes. I didn't even turn on the light because I didn't want anyone to see where I was.

In the darkness, I suddenly heard a familiar voice. It was

the missions chairwoman of the largest missions church in New England. A great saint, she was listing names and claiming these people for world evangelization. She and God were recruiting.

Afterwards I asked her who she was praying for. "All the young people in our church between the ages of ten and sixteen," she said. "I've committed myself to the Lord to pray that God would call many of them from our church to serve him overseas." She had been doing this ever since she had come on the missions board at her church. At that point, about 250 people had gone out from families in that church.

And then she said, "Tom, are you praying for the young people here at this church? I think it's part of your job." That was a few years ago, and I did begin praying!

But let me tell you something else about the importance of prayer. When I was one of those ten-to-sixteen year olds in my church, I was a hellion. I was a bad kid and I'm not proud of it. But I knew there were three older ladies in my church who prayed for me faithfully, whether I liked it or not. The three of them had all spent some time on the mission field themselves. Those three ladies were the first to respond to my letters when I announced that I was going full time with ACMC. One of them, Gladys, wrote and said she was going to send me five dollars per month because God had answered her prayers. Well, her five dollars didn't mean nearly as much as her prayers.

Once I visited these three elderly saints who were all in

> *There were three older ladies in my church who prayed for me faithfully when I was a rebellious teenager, whether I liked it or not.*

senior citizen homes nearby. I went to see Gladys first. I knocked on the door and she could barely see. I said, "Gladys, do you know who this is?" She said, "Tommy!" and gave me a big hug. As we talked, I asked her what she did all day. She said, "Come here and I'll show you." She had an old yellow legal pad with fifty-two names of missionaries written down. "I spend my day praying for these people. See, Tommy, here's your name."

I walked out to my car that day and cried half the way home. If God is accomplishing anything in my ministry today, that's the reason. We must be committed to recruiting missionaries through prayer and to supporting them through prayer.

FAN FARE

Amateur Umpire

In our small town, parents from each Little League team served as umpire and referree. It so happened one day that I was the only parent present at my son's game. The coach turned to me and said, "Well, I guess you're it."

"But I've never done this before," I protested.

"Well, you know the rules, don't you?"

Yes, I knew the rules, at least the common ones. So it was settled. The father from the other team said, "I'll call the outs at home plate, you call them in the field." Sounded good to me.

"Where do I stand?" I asked. He motioned, "About here if the bases are empty, and out here if someone is on base."

Aside from feeling a bit awkward standing out in the field, things went pretty smoothly. I was really enjoying the game, when suddenly there was a close play at second base. While I was realizing I was supposed to call the play and deciding what to call, I heard someone call "Out!" I assumed it was the plate umpire, and since obviously the referees should agree, I immediately bawled, "Out!"

"Don't let the *coach* call 'em," someone yelled at me from the bleachers.

Later in the game with the other team at bat, a similar close play occurred. Immediately I yelled "Out!"

"Well, at least he's consistent," grumbled the person in the bleachers.

—*David Mays, Great Lakes Regional Director, ACMC*

3
Spring Training

Improving Your Missions Training Program

"We teach what we know; we reproduce what we are."

The best high school baseball team I ever umpired for was at St. James High School in Chester, Pennsylvania. At the time I was Commissioner of the Catholic High School League in Philadelphia, and I was umpiring a lot. One day I arrived at St. James early and the whole team was there on the bench, waiting for the game to start. Strangely enough, I didn't see their coach anywhere. So I went over to the guys and asked, "Where's Coach John?"

They said, "We don't know. He must have been in a car accident, or he'd be here."

You know what? It turned out to be true—their coach *had* been in a car accident, and he didn't show up until the fourth inning. His absence didn't affect his players' behavior though. Those guys went out and did exactly what he would have wanted them to do.

Coach Mooney was one of the finest coaches in the city of Philadelphia. It wasn't just that one game that convinced me.

I'd seen John quietly take one guy aside, put his arm around his shoulder and talk to him. I'd seen him take another guy and publicly mock him. Somehow he knew his team—who needed a kick in the pants and who needed a pat on the shoulder. And like any good coach, he stuck with the fundamentals. The St. James team was successful because of the quality of its trainer.

> *The best missions trainers are trainable themselves. They never stop learning, never stop seeking advice.*

Likewise, the bottom line in any good missions training program in the church is dependent on who is doing the teaching and training. The training is only as good as the trainer, so that's where churches need to start in getting their missions programs off the ground. As I always say, we teach what we know, but we reproduce what we are.

What qualities of a good coach would be transferable to a trainer in missions?

In many ways good coaching qualities are useful in any kind of training you do. I see three top traits that good coaches will exhibit.

First, coaches model what they want done. They don't just talk about it; they do it. You can always tell what kind of a model a coach is by looking at his team. If a team carries on all the time, clashing with an umpire, it's probably because the coach carries on.

Second, coaches know how to handle people (including themselves). Good coaches, like John Mooney, listen well and seek out the best way to handle individuals and the team as a whole. Such coaches are able to tell that someone like me could handle (and benefit from) being made fun of in front of people, but that such treatment would never work with another team member.

Third, coaches are trainable. The best coaches are willing to keep on learning. They never stop seeking advice, new ideas, and ways to improve.

In my own life and continuing development as a missions trainer, I've seen the importance of these qualities. I have been blessed with some great role models and mentors. Dave Mays was a successful chemist who got turned on to missions. He left his job, went to Wheaton Graduate School, and joined the staff of ACMC. Dave shares everything he learns with me. He gives me his stuff and doesn't care who gets the credit. He tells me what books to read. He challenges me to think through new ideas.

I like to hang around with very smart people. I speak at seminars with Christian leaders such as Tony Campolo, John Piper, Ralph Winter, Don Richardson, Harvie Conn, and other missions gurus. I have learned to shut up and listen. I like to see what works, to see how they teach and motivate.

Sometimes these mentors have gone beyond providing a model for me to watch and have given me personal insights based on their understanding of my specific needs. I used to always apologize for my lack of education when I would get up to speak. Then one day Ralph Winter came up to me after I had given a seminar and said, "If I hear you talk about your lack of education again, I'll see if I can get you fired." He wanted me to accept what God had done in my life and not apologize for it. It was a chance for me to see a great trainer in action, and he has certainly influenced my life.

For some reason, the idea of being trainable clicked with me when I started training umpires at my school. I had seen the youth pastor at our church using overheads in teaching, so I went to him and asked him to help me make some of those things and teach me how you use the machine. I wanted to do it right. He also helped me make a magnetic board, and we painted a baseball diamond on it. With the umpires, I'd go through the drills on the board first and then we'd go outside and do them. I did this at two or three colleges in the Philadelphia area, and a couple of college scouts saw me teach and put these guys in learning situations. "We've never done it this way before," the scouts said. (Almost sounds like church, eh?) So, it got around Philadelphia that if you wanted to be a good umpire, you needed to go see Tom Telford.

This is also what got me into the big leagues—the big league people saw me teaching the skills. But everything I taught I learned at Major League Umpire School or I learned by watching what worked. I'm not original, just teachable.

I did not start out teachable, however. When I was growing up, I never stuck at anything. I was thrown out of school many times because I wasn't teachable, and finally quit in tenth grade. It is so encouraging to look back and see how God has changed me into a more teachable person. The process was under way when I began training umpires, and it continues today.

Several years ago Dr. Hulbert, then the provost of Columbia International University, asked me to fill in as an adjunct professor for Paul Borthwick, author of many missions books. He said, "Tom, just put a syllabus together of what you want to do, and we'll go with it." I couldn't tell him then that I didn't know what a syllabus was or what an adjunct professor was! But my experience teaching there has been good from the beginning.

More recently, I went to teach a two-hour seminar to missions leadership at a church in Charlottesville, Virginia. I guess you could say it's a church with a high percentage of intellectuals. (Their pastor, for example, had graduated first in his class at Harvard.) I had had a few hard weeks in ministry before that, and I was feeling my shortcomings, ready to throw in the glove. That wasn't God's game plan for me, though. After I taught that seminar, a guy in the church came up to me and said, "Tom, that's some of the best teaching I've sat under."

I said, "Yeah, is that so?" (I wasn't in the mood for this). He said, "Yeah, that's so. And I should know about teaching because I've been voted the top teacher in the University of Virginia three years running."

When he finished talking, I cried. I told him, "I've been going through some tough times and I was deciding to hang it up." This guy encouraged me to keep going and then he wrote me a very encouraging letter. God knows when to pat us on the back. I'm telling you all this because I want to make this point very strongly. When I became trainable, God used me.

On the local church and missions scene, things are moving quickly. Things are changing. A good missions trainer needs to be always hungry to learn so he or she can coach the team with as much information and as many new ideas as possible. A trainable missions trainer absolutely has to be a reader. You don't have to know everything; you just need to know more next year, or next month, than you do now. I read all the time. I have a lot of guys around me who keep feeding me books, and I keep feeding books to

> *Missions is changing as fast as computer science is changing. In the twenty-first century it will be a whole new ball game. We've got to keep up.*

others. Missions is changing as fast as computer science is changing. In the twenty-first century it will be a whole new ball game. We've got to keep up.

Let me give you a more specific short list of what I see as qualities of the person who is going to lead and educate church members in the area of missions. This is either the missions chairperson or someone else on the missions committee who is especially gifted in training.

1. Missions trainers must have enthusiasm. You have to believe 200 percent in what you're doing. You have to believe that world evangelization is at the center of God's heart, that it is the theme of God's Word, and that it is the mandate of the church.

2. Missions trainers must have discipline. J. Oswald Sanders said, "He is able to lead because he has conquered himself." My biggest problem has always been myself. Trainers need to be humble, develop spiritual disciplines, and ask God to help them grow in love and self-control and other fruit of the Spirit.

3. Missions trainers must have vision. When I was with ACMC, we had a goal to help 6,000 churches mobilize by the year 2000. That requires vision. I remember being in a prayer meeting many years ago with Ralph Winter who shared his vision for an interdenominational research and resource agency for missions. As we prayed for his dream, I think he was the only person in the room who believed it would happen. And God did eventually answer his prayer with the founding of the U. S. Center for World Mission. What kind of vision do you have for your church? Do you think you can recruit, train, and send out a missionary, even if you never have before? Do you believe you could double your missions budget in the next five years? Having the vision is the place to start.

4. Missions trainers must have wisdom to see God's heart for the world. If you haven't got this, what will keep you going when the training gets tough? I'll never forget being encouraged in this area through a paper written by one of my students at Columbia International University. She said:

> My Bible oozes with missions. I think I must have a special Bible because other people don't seem to think their Bibles ooze. Or maybe it's because my Bible has transformed itself over the years, because now that I think about it, my Bible seems to talk a lot more about missions now than it did five years ago.
>
> Well, I know that God's Word doesn't change, and I know that there are not multiple versions of the same translation. Could it be then, that I have changed? That must be it. Maybe even more about missions is written in the Word than I can see now. I guess God will continue to reveal more of his heart for the world as I continue to seek him. How exciting life is with God.

5. Missions trainers must be good decision makers. Good decision making involves having the courage to stand against emotional decision making. This is not always easy. The Holy Spirit doesn't zap us with the right answer. Sometimes we're wrong; sometimes we're right.

I remember one time when a team of eighteen high school students were going from our church to do a work project in Haiti. We had narrowed the list of participants down through the training program, but there was one kid on that team who I really thought should not go, and some of the other church leaders agreed with me. He was one of those kids who wore jeans that you buy with the holes already in them and it costs more for the holes. We didn't like his attitude, or the way he treated his mother. All of his support came in, however, and he finished rather rigorous training. We made the hard decision and let him go on the project. He was the only one on the team who could play the guitar, and we needed music in the church where they were going. Maybe that was a weak reason. His mother told me he loved his guitar more than he loved her.

Off went the team, and we did a lot of praying.

A few weeks later we met them all at the airport, and that night they led the Sunday evening service. When this kid went up to the front of the church to lead the meeting, a hush fell over everyone. I think we were all wondering what on earth he would say. He told us he had left his guitar in Haiti because the church didn't have one. He told us how he taught a kid to play the guitar. He said he left all his designer jeans and came home with an empty suitcase. He told us how he met Jesus on that trip. Proof positive that God can use situations in people's lives even when we aren't sure we've made the right decision.

> *Good decision making involves having the courage to stand against emotional decision making. We have to ask for God's grace, boldly make a decision, and then follow through.*

6. *Missions trainers must be humble.* People who train others well are humble enough to allow people to try. I remember being with a friend of mine who was a missionary home on furlough. This guy was a seminary professor with a Ph.D. We were in a little church, sitting in a men's Sunday school class, and the layman who was teaching wasn't doing a very good job. But here was this seasoned missionary teacher listening

intently, never criticizing or correcting, and only answering a question when he was called on. He didn't show the teacher up—he even made him look a bit better. People will accept training from this kind of a guy.

7. *Missions trainers must have a sense of humor.* And the laughter has to start with yourself. You can't take yourself too seriously. The missions committees I have worked with could tell you a lot of stories on me. I learn by making lots of mistakes. If I couldn't laugh, I'd be finished.

What should a good overall training program look like in the local church?

Training must start early.
Start doing missions teaching and training in pre-school. Teach the toddlers about great superheroes of the faith. The reason I am in missions today is partly because as a small child I was taught about missionaries by my parents and my Sunday school teachers. I knew who Adoniram Judson and William Carey were. I loved to hear about Hudson Taylor. These guys were my heroes.

Do missions training in preschool. Teach the toddlers about great missionary heroes of the faith.

I was recently teaching at a conference for teachers of Christian schools. I won't tell you where. There were 250 teachers there from evangelical churches. I asked them to raise their hands if they knew who the founder of modern missions was. You know how many raised their hands? Thirteen. What a tragedy. (And by the way, these are the Christian schools that a lot of churches put in their missions budget for support. It's fine to support them, but don't put it under missions—especially if there is absolutely no missions teaching going on in the schools.)

I made the mistake of challenging one church I was visiting about starting early and training the children. As I was going out the door, a dear woman came up to me and said, "Tom, I see that you're going to be with us for the next three Sundays, so I would like you to teach our toddler department about missions." *Me and my big mouth,* I thought. In the airport, on the way home, I saw six nice carved elephants, and I thought I could use them. I called the woman and got the names of the missionaries that church supported in Africa, six of them, and I put one name on the back of each elephant. I also asked the woman to put a big map of Africa on the wall.

When I returned, by the end of those three weeks the toddlers knew the names of those six missionaries, knew they were in Africa telling people about Jesus, and had begun praying for them. That was my first experience with toddlers, but they can do it!

> *Train missionary candidates at home first. If they can't plant a church in Boston, how are they going to plant one in Bosnia?*

Training must begin at home first.

You don't get zapped with the "missionary gift" when you get on an airplane. Short-term missions training programs and neighborhood programs can train people, and they can be used to screen out people who are not missionary material. I would never invest thousands of dollars in sending people overseas to plant churches if they had never been involved in planting a church here in America. If they can't plant a church in Boston, how are they going to plant one in Bosnia?

I can think of a really significant example of home training for one of our missionaries in our church. A missionary had been preparing to go overseas for some time. He was a pilot trained at JAARS, the Wycliffe flight school, and had taken his required Bible courses. He and his family had all their support raised and just needed the OK from the missions committee. They were ready to go. The only snag was that this missionary had never led anyone to the Lord. One of our "train at home first" requirements was that before you went overseas, you needed to demonstrate that you could lead someone to faith in the Lord.

Well, this guy was upset with me and so were some of the people on the missions committee. He said, "I'm going to be a pilot. I'm in a support ministry. Why is this so necessary?"

Time went on and this guy still hadn't led anyone to the Lord. His patience was wearing thin. But one night, this missionary was with some young people doing evangelism out at the airport, and he led someone to Christ! Off he went to the mission field, but within a short time he was grounded from flying for physical reasons. He ended up doing evangelism and leading Bible studies. He wrote me and said how thankful he was that he had been trained in evangelism before he left.

I believe you must demonstrate your worthiness at home, before you go overseas. It's a must.

I was talking about this whole concept in my home church. After I had been going on about knowing how to do evangelism at home before you go overseas and about teaching children when they are young, one of the Vacation Bible School teachers stopped me. She asked me to put my money where my mouth was and teach a group of kids at the Vacation Bible School.

So, I had a table of seven kids about seven and eight years old. There was a little girl who didn't have her Bible, and she missed out on getting the five points for bringing a Bible. When I asked where her Bible was, she said she didn't have one. The next day, though, she brought one. When the children went out for recess, I checked her copy out and saw it had been checked out of the public library! Well, the girl accepted the Lord that week at Bible school.

I made it through Vacation Bible School—even weathering the storm of daily handcraft time for a whole week. I felt pretty good and was patting myself on the back for a job well done. Then I got a letter from that sharp woman who headed up the department saying, "Tom, your job is not done. Go and call on the kids at your table who accepted Jesus as their Savior. Call on them at their homes."

I'm too busy for that, I thought. I was driving off to Princeton Seminary to do an ACMC seminar. I said, *Lord, I'm busy calling on churches—I don't have to do that!"*

But the letter was still there on the car seat beside me, and all of a sudden I realized I was stopped at a traffic light at the very street where this eight year old lived. I'm no different than anybody else—I'm scared to go and pound on people's doors when I don't know them. But I went and knocked at the door, and the little girl answered and smiled up at me. Such a cute little girl. She ran and got her mother. When her mother came out, I said, "Hello, I'm Tom Telford. I taught your daughter last week at Vacation Bible School." We talked about the weather and everything else I could think of. Finally I said, "Do you know what your daughter did last week? She accepted Jesus Christ as her Savior!"

And you know what that woman said to me? (I am not making this up.) She said, "And who in h— is Jesus Christ?" This woman said she had never had a Bible in her hand, and the only thing she knew about Jesus was that it was a swear word. She lived near our church. Later, I walked out of that house and got back in my car realizing that the mission field is everywhere. We can be trained right where we are.

Training must involve the whole congregation.

I think one of our biggest problems in the American church is self-centeredness. How much of the church's finances go to things that somehow benefit the membership themselves?

For example, our church decided to spend $70,000 to fix up the fellowship hall. It was okayed by the congregation in 92 seconds. If I had asked for $70,000 to reach an unreached people group, would they have given it to me in 92 seconds? I don't think so. I think we would have argued for nine weeks on that one. And I don't think my church is any different than most. We're all selfish.

Your church won't have a heart for world evangelization if people think the "great commission" is about a sales incentive for Wal-Mart employees.

We also have a low image of missionaries. Sometimes people tell me that missionaries go overseas because they can't hack it over here. The average Christian is illiterate when it comes to missions. Your church won't have a heart for world evangelization if your people think the "great commission" is about a sales incentive for Wal-Mart employees. These are attitudes that need training and retraining.

Training must involve the pastor.

You'll never find a missions-minded church without a missions-minded pastor. One pastor I know told me, "I'm missions-minded. I preach two missions messages a year." Well, that's not enough. Why don't we have more pastors at our national missions conferences? They are at Promise Keepers and pastors' seminars aren't they? An even more important way to train pastors and to get them excited about missions is to send them to the mission field. (If you don't like him or her, buy a one-way ticket!)

Sending your pastor overseas is an optimum plan in three ways. It educates the pastor; it allows him to encourage the missionaries; and it gives him first-hand knowledge of needs and challenges that he can share with the church.

Pastors are often more ignorant of missions than opposed to it. In many of our leading Bible colleges, there are no required missions courses for pastors. I have found only two courses, anywhere, for future pastors on how to lead a local church in missions.

One school that is an exception to that is Columbia International University. Columbia has a big sign you see when you come on to campus that says, "To know Christ and to make Him known." You can't be on that campus long without thinking of missions. Once when I was speaking in chapel there I said, "This college reeks of missions." Dr. McQuilken, the past president, later told me, "Tom, I think the word you want is *ethos.*" So what I mean is there's a missions ethos at Columbia. He also showed me a letter he had received that said: "I'm sending my two sons to your school. Make missionaries out of them." Dr. McQuilken said, "We don't make missionaries here; the church does. We help train and smooth off the rough edges, but the church makes missionaries." If he is right about the church's role, then pastors definitely need to be trained in missions.

Training must involve all the leaders.
Here's a question to ask the missions committee, the Sunday school teachers, and the elders and deacons: "Who are you

discipling for missions this year?" Send them a note with that question on it. See what happens.

I believe that one of the mandates for a healthy church is that the leaders and teachers need to disciple our people to be involved in world evangelization. Not just a few unusual people are called. We need to be called to stay as much as called to go. Obedience to the great commission must have top priority for all of us.

> *We need to be called to stay as much as called to go. Obedience to the great commission must have top priority for all of us.*

Training must include teenagers and senior adults.

We need to remember what we said when we dedicated our babies to the Lord—that we would give our children back to him. Teenagers should be in good missions training programs. The need to take part in vision trips or short-term ministry trips. They can learn how to lead someone to Christ. Why do we usually only recruit adults for evangelism seminars?

By the way, I would never send a kid to Haiti on a youth missions trip if he or she couldn't lead someone to Christ. No matter what they are planning to do on such a trip, they need to know the most important thing of all: how to tell lost people about Jesus.

On the other end of the spectrum are the older saints. I got tired of seeing the seniors in our church go on these scenic tours, trips to outlet malls, and outings to the shore. Too often we forget what a valuable resource the senior population is to the church. Once I said to the pastor for the seniors, "I think these people would feel a lot better if they did something worthwhile on these outings." He said, "OK, Tom, you come up with the ideas." So I wrote to three mission agencies that were within reach and asked them if they had a job that fifty people could work on for a day.

A month later, our seniors all got onto a bus and went to Overseas Missionary Fellowship to stuff envelopes and help get a mailing out. Some of those dear old people came to me afterwards and said, "Tom, that was great. We want to go back on our own and help them." A few more people involved in missions!

I know of senior individuals who have taken on the challenge of missions in amazing ways. Once in an airport in Pittsburgh, an elderly woman came up to me and said, "You're Tom Telford! I was just in your workshop. Guess what I'm doing? I just retired from AT&T, I have a great pension, and I'm going to be a missionary nanny. I have the money, so I can do it. I heard about these young couples who go to language school and have difficulty because they need help with the children when they are in classes. So I volunteered to be a nanny."

Then she told me that when she got home she was going to use her administrative gifts to organize a ministry called Missionary Nannies. I have since seen her ads in missions magazines and this retired grandmother's organization has really taken off and grown.

Seniors can be great support personnel. A missionary friend of mine knew a woman in his congregation who was an executive secretary. She went overseas to his field office and completely set up and computerized his office for him. What a service! There are so many people who could do things like that. The Bible says the old should teach the young, but what do too many of us do? We retire. Forget that. Do what you enjoy as you serve the Lord. Take a risk. Get out of your comfort zone.

Training and retraining must never stop.

The Sunday school teachers, elders, deacons, and women's ministries personnel all need to see missions not as just another program in the church, vying for the people's attention and resources, but as the umbrella under which all the other ministries work. With missions as such an integral part of the church's focus, each member of the congregation must keep on learning. As my friend Carl Palmer says, "Time sharpening the axe is never wasted." I hope we as church leaders will never get to a point where we don't even notice if our axes are dull.

Baseball provides a good example of what we need. I know Pete Rose has had his problems, but I really admired him when I was working in Philadelphia because he worked so hard. He would come early and hit 300 balls. He just wouldn't quit. And then I'd look over at some of those young hotshot players whose names you'll never remember, and they would be sitting goofing off.

To keep improving your missions training game, you have to work hard at the basics, be a good model, and hunger to grow and learn yourself. For me, this means, in part, listening to people, picking their brains, learning from them, and passing it on.

Cross-Cultural Baseball

Like a lot of things that Americans export overseas, baseball is hard to explain.

In 1993, when my wife and I were returning home from a trip in Africa, an American friend in Switzerland invited us to join her for a "real American barbecue" in Switzerland. Part of the activity was a baseball game, which I was called upon to explain—through a translator.

Well, the game got under way . . . sort of.

"But I thought you said if I hit the ball out into the field, I could run around the bases and make a home run?"

"Yes, but not if the guy out there catches it! You're out!"

"That's not fair!"

"Maybe not, but that's baseball."

Later, as I was about to wind up for a pitch, I noticed that there were two runners on second base at the same time. I thought to myself, *Is that really so bad? Is it worth another translated argument? Ah, who cares? Play ball.*

We were playing women against men. The guys had but one objective when they were at bat: try to hit the ball as hard as they could because every hit had to be a home run. So in no time, the women were way ahead of us.

When we finally stopped, everyone seemed happy, though we had overlooked or broken lots of rules. But perhaps those rules weren't all that important at a French-speaking baseball game in Switzerland. I learned more about cross-cultural understanding in that one game than I did in two weeks of mission orientation school: It's not whether you win or lose, it's whether you have any friends when it's all over!

—Ken Wiley, missionary engineer with AIM

4
Play Ball!

Tips for Effective Missions Conferences

> "If saving a lost world is so important
> to God, then the missions conference
> should be the highlight of the church
> year."

The great sportswriter Thomas Boswell wrote a book with a title that says it all: *Time Begins on Opening Day*. The excitement, fervor, and anticipation of a season opener is almost a religious experience for many baseball lovers. The high feeling I get on the first day of a missions conference is very much like what I might feel at an opening day in baseball.

How do you suggest igniting a similar excitement for missions conferences in congregations?

Extending the above comparison, a missions conference is like opening day in baseball because it sets the tone, the momentum, and the energy for a church's whole year in missions. I can't say too strongly how committed I am to missions conferences in the church. Here are some tips for getting the support you need and pulling together effective, electrifying missions conferences.

Make sure your leadership is backing you.

I have one thing I want to say right off: If your pastor doesn't take your conference seriously—fire him! That may sound a bit strong, but I mean it. When I was missions chairman once, the pastor called me into his office two weeks before the missions conference and said, "Tom, I'm going away for the week of the missions conference. You've got everything well-planned, and I'm exhausted. I need a break."

You know what I said to him? I said, "Pastor, if you do that, I'm going to the elders and will ask for your resignation. Do you have any idea what that single act says to your people about the importance you place on world evangelization?"

He stayed.

You see, as the pastor goes, so goes the church. I pestered that pastor a lot, but we had a positive relationship. Unfortunately, it can be a big challenge to get pastors turned on to missions. That is still hard for me to understand. If the mandate of the local church is to do world evangelization, how can someone possibly graduate from a theological seminary or school that trains pastors and know nothing about missions?

As the pastor goes, so goes the church.

Send pastors on missions trips to open their eyes and raise their enthusiasm. I frequently give pastors books on missions. Then I call them a few weeks later and ask them what chapter they are reading. They're on to me now, so they read them! Missions committee people need to encourage their pastor when it comes to missions. Feed them information. Be their coach in learning about missions.

Make the conference the absolute highlight of the church year.

Even above Christmas or Easter. God is a missionary God. Jesus was his missionary Son. The Bible is a missionary book. The Old Testament is packed with God's heart for the nations. The New Testament mandate for the believer is to go into all the world and make disciples. I can't imagine why any other single event in the church should have more importance than the celebration of the calling of the church to reach the lost. If saving a lost world is so important to God, then the missions conference should be the highlight of the church year.

Let me explain why this needs so much emphasis. Once I was at a large, well-known Bible college speaking on missions. I said to the students, "I'm going to call out a word, and you fire back the first things that come into your head." They were up for it, so I yelled, "Missions!" Answers came back fast and furious: "pith helmet" . . . "snake stories" . . . "horrible slides" . . . "used tea bags" . . . "out-of-date" . . . "boring." They gave about eight answers before I got anything positive from that crowd.

Where did they get those images? From dull missions conferences. Some of our missions conferences are a disgrace. They paint such a drab picture of missions. They're uncreative, poorly planned, and predictable—the same old thing year after year.

The year I became missions chairman in our church, I went to the previous chairman and asked him for his notes. He brought out a notebook with the last twenty-seven conferences outlined in it. As I began to look through it, a horrible realization came over me—every single conference was exactly the same. Do you know what we did? We canceled the conference that year. We tried to figure out what we should be doing.

In some churches, the missions conference is the one event people won't miss. Another measure of their success is that they win over people who are not in the missions camp. One thing is certain: the attitude in these churches is not, "Well, it's the third week of October so get out the flags and we'll do the missions thing for a week." Rather, they are sold out to making the conference the highlight it can be.

Plan the conference well in advance and avoid conflicts.

Don't hold the missions conference on the weekend of the Super Bowl. You need to meet with all the other ministries in the church and be sure that all the other programs get integrated into the missions celebration. Don't have competition.

> *Get everyone involved. Include fun missions activities in Sunday school or do a missions musical. Why should Christmas and Easter get all the music?*

Involve all the programs in the church. If you have sharp Christian education people or a vital Pioneer Clubs or women's ministries program, dip the groups into missions and soak them. Get your creative Christian education people to put on some fun learning activities or your choir to do a missions musical. Why should Christmas and Easter get all the music? Involve all the other church ministries. People will come if their children are in a missions play or if their relatives or friends are in a missions drama or musical event.

Settle for nothing less than excellent, creative, classy publicity and promotion.
Try your best to put out really good promotion. If you produce something in one color on an old copy machine in the church basement, you might as well print on the flier, "Missions is dull and boring." Find someone in your church who has the necessary gifts or hire a local Christian artist. Get ideas from other people. Check your mailbox for classy mailings. With computers these days, printing doesn't have to be expensive to do a high-quality job. Surprise your people with your promotion.

Think of creative new names. Instead of calling it a missions conference, try one of these: World Fest, World Expo, Harvest Celebration, Global Awareness Week. Remember that most baby boomers and busters are turned off by the word *missions*.

Look at what other churches do. If you see another church doing a great job, call them up and find out what they are doing well.

Collect brochures at conferences. ACMC displays good ideas from all over the country at their conferences. Often the ideas you can pick up from other churches are worth the cost of participating in these conferences. ACMC publishes some handbooks with ideas as well. One year I took a pile of self-addressed, stamped envelopes to the ACMC national conference. When people shared a great idea or told me about something their church did, I gave them an envelope and asked them to send me a copy when they got home.

Get kids to help with promotion. I remember one "Missions Moment" during our church's Sunday morning worship. The committee had a little girl get up say, "Hooray! It's two weeks to the missions conference!" Then she proceeded to list off from memory our thirty-three missionaries and the countries they served in. When she was done, the congregation cheered.

Whatever you do, get the best people and do it better than any other program in the church. Make people wish they were on the missions committee because it does things so well.

Secure top speakers for the conference.
Your speaker should be as good as, or better than, your pastor. Bring in third-world Christian leaders to expose your people to international speakers. For some of these leaders, this requires booking a couple of years in advance (one of the many reasons you need to plan conferences as far ahead as possible).

Use your missionaries during the conference.
Believe it or not, I go to missions conferences that don't have missionaries present! On the other hand, make sure you find a good fit for the missionary. If a person is not a good speaker, don't put him or her in the pulpit. That's one situation where those bad images of missionaries come from. Just because someone doesn't speak well before an American audience, it doesn't mean he or she is not a good missionary. Have some missionaries speak to small gatherings, or at coffee times in homes. Put them where they do best.

Even in my rebellious teen years, I respected missionaries because I had watched them in our home, and I had heard them tell stories that made my hair stand on end. They were heroes to me because my parents made them a part of our lives. So put those missionaries in the homes of people who need to get excited about missions, not in the homes of the people on the missions committee. That's just preaching to the choir.

Don't leave children out of the conference.
Spend as much time and money on the children as you do

on the adults. Once when I was speaking at a banquet for retiring and retired missionaries, I asked each one of the people present to stand up and tell me at what age he or she became interested in being a missionary. For about 80 percent of them, their interest began when they were under the age of twelve. So don't put all the young people in the basement, give them pizza, let them watch a Disney movie, and then wonder why they are not turned on to world missions.

There are lots of resources available for missions mobilization with youth. The U.S. Center for World Mission has a Children's Mission Resource Center (1605 Elizabeth St. Pasadena, CA. 91104). Jan Bell heads up an organization called Kidscan Network, and offers a catalog with tons of great ideas for having a terrific children's conference (4445 Webster Dr., Yonkers, PA, 17402). ACMC offers resources through M & M Kids (call 800-607-3783). If we leave out our kids, we're missing the boat in a big way.

Incorporate faith-promise giving into your conference.

A faith promise is committing to giving a certain amount over and above a tithe as an act of faith. I believe starting such a practice is one way to energize the missions giving in the church and also to energize the conference itself. Not everyone agrees with me on this, but I believe it has lots of advantages, mainly that it teaches the congregation how to live by faith.

The faith-promise idea was made prominent by A. B. Simpson, who founded the Christian Missionary Alliance around 1900. He formulated it from verses that were promises based on faith, especially 2 Corinthians 8:1-2 where it says the believers gave beyond their resources.

At various conferences I have often asked pastors, "How many of you have 100 percent of your people tithing?" No hands go up. So I ask, "90 percent? 80 percent? 70? 60?" Once in a while there's a hand that comes up at 40 percent, but usually about 20 percent of most congregations are actually tithing. The faith-promise program is designed to get people to give over and above their tithes, and that's pretty difficult if you don't even have them tithing. But I have seen it work. It requires solid teaching to keep people mindful and motivated, but I believe it is biblical.

Stuart Briscoe, who has pastored Elmbrook Church in Wisconsin for many years, writes:

> When I came to Elmbrook, one of the first things I asked was how much they gave to missions each year. They said, "Oh, our mission is to Milwaukee."
>
> I said, "No, how much do you give to missions?"
> "About $12,000."
>
> I was afraid to ask whether that was a week or a month. But to my horror I found out it was per year. They noticed that my face fell, so they stuttered and said, "What should we do?"
>
> We doubled it each year for the next four years and the church barely noticed it. In the fourth year, I talked to the congregation about the fact that although missionaries have to exercise faith, we at home can usually get by without exercising faith. That's not fair. Why should we send missionaries out into the middle of nowhere with no visible means of support and expect them to do their job, while we sit at home knowing where every penny is coming from? A faith promise program gives everybody an opportunity to exercise faith.

Briscoe went on to suggest that each member go home and pray, asking God to help them trust him for a certain amount more than what they knew they could count on or expect—with the goal of advancing world evangelization.

I think a faith promise gives everybody the chance to be involved in learning to trust. It gives people who are in a comfortable, predictable, organized, structured lifestyle the opportunity to go out on a limb of faith, to take a risk. I think of a man in my church who once gave me $1,000 cash for missions. It was a wonderful gift, but he didn't know what faith promise was about at all. He had the money in the bank. It didn't take any faith at all to give me money he had handy. I feel sorry for people who live ordered, safe lives because they never know the exhilarating feeling of stepping out in faith.

> *Faith-promise giving to missions gives people who are in a comfortable, predictable, lifestyle the opportunity to go out on a limb of faith.*

They can manage without ever learning to trust. They need to make a faith promise.

Let me tell you another story of a ten-year-old boy I'll call Jack. His father had been a missionary who was killed in China, and his mother worked for OMF. A few weeks after our faith-promise commitments at the end of our missions conference, Jack came to me and said, "Mr. Telford, I want my card back. I don't have the money I promised."

I said, "I don't think you've given God enough time to work and get that ten dollars you put down there."

So, over the next few weeks when he came to church he'd find me and say, "I don't have it yet!" We'd pray together and ask God to meet his faith promise. As the year wound down, I was afraid my young friend was not going to secure the money he had promised to give. I was tempted to write him a check myself. Then one night Jack called me and exclaimed, "Mr. Telford, I've been out shoveling snow and I have $22.50 for my faith promise!" He was so excited! As I calculate it, that's double what he promised God by faith.

Jack and his mother moved away, but about eight years later I ran into Jack again. Here was this big, tall guy who gave me a big hug and said, "Thanks for helping me learn a lesson about faith when I was a little boy. That's why I'm going into missions today. I want to keep learning to learn to trust God."

Get people personally involved with the missionaries you support.

We need to care for our missionaries. In baby-boomer lingo this is called creating "high touch" between the missionary and the church people. All of us are more committed to things we get involved with and invest in.

We can provide counseling for missionaries, take them shopping, organize a food shower for them, extend hospitality. A missions conference is the perfect place to make those connections and involvements happen.

One time at the end of our missions conference I had one of my crazy ideas of getting congregation members involved. It was Sunday morning and I stood up and said, "How many people in this church are going to another part of the world this summer for vacation? How many will cross the ocean? Raise your hands." About fifteen people raised their hands. I had a spy in the balcony write all their names down and where they said they were going. Then we tried to connect each of them with a missionary who was located in that area. We called this a "vacation with a purpose." If they are going overseas anyway, why not visit missionaries and encourage them?

There was a man in our church who some of us in leadership privately called "Fast Harry" because he always came into church at five minutes to eleven and left at five to twelve, no matter whether the pastor was finished or not. Well, Fast Harry was one of those who raised his hand that he was going overseas. So I decided to encourage him to visit a missionary. This was a guy who only came to church one hour a week, and not a whole lot of people even knew him.

Fast Harry was going to France, and I wanted him to visit a very sharp couple of missionaries who were planting a church outside of Paris. He said he couldn't do it and that he would be in a very different part of France. He was quite negative. But I was ready with two Eurorail passes which you could get from travel agents at that time. I said, "Here are two rail passes so we can make this possible," and before he could say no, I handed him the passes, bowed my head, and started praying that he'd have a successful trip.

> *Take a "vacation with a purpose." If you are going overseas anyway, why not visit missionaries and encourage them?*

Then in September we had our usual men's missionary breakfast with a speaker and a challenge for the year, and in came Fast Harry. The pastor kicked me under the table and I almost dropped my teeth. Fast Harry on a Saturday morning! After the missionary spoke, we threw it open for sharing, and the first guy on his feet was Fast Harry. He told how he had gone to visit two of our missionaries who were church planting in Paris. Right away he had been asked to help set up chairs in a storefront church. He said, "And then I heard them singing familiar hymns in a language I didn't understand and praying with such joy." Before Harry was done describing his experience, there were tears running down his face. At the prayer time he got up and prayed for those misionaries. I found out later that it was his first time to pray publicly. Missions conferences do change lives.

There are countless ways to encourage personal involvement with missionaries.

1. If someone in your church has a lovely home, have the person invite eight or ten ladies over for coffee and cheesecake and have one of your senior missionaries come and share her life experiences. She will probably do wonderfully in that setting, whereas in the pulpit, she may not do well at all.

2. What about a man who is a builder or does agricultural projects overseas? Have a men's breakfast where he can talk hardware and "Home Improvement" and be appreciated for it.

3. Have a talent night for your missionaries and let missionaries who want to show the people another side of them. The daughter of one of our missionaries did ballet to a Scripture chorus in a women's meeting. The women thoroughly enjoyed it, and it certainly broke some stereotypes of missionaries.

4. Once we got a busload of guys as well as all the male missionaries at the conference, and we all went down to a Phillies baseball game in Philadelphia. All the way to the game and all the way back, the men chatted with the missionaries and got to know them as regular guys. Some of those relationships have lasted until today.

5. A women's version of that was when our church took all the women missionaries, plus our ladies, on three buses to a great outlet mall nearby. Those ladies talked all the way there and back, stopped for lunch at the mall, and shopped

till they dropped. You can be sure some lifetime friendships with missionaries were born on that shopping trip. People pray for people they know and for people they have invested some of their own lives and time with.

Evaluate your conference and see how to make it better.

When it's all over, talk about what worked and what didn't. Maybe your people are tired of ethnic dinners with flags from around the world stuck in their Jell-O salad. Maybe they don't notice the banners anymore, or maybe the missions committee has not been integrating its ministry with all the programs of the church. Are the people tired of snake stories, fuzzy slides, and guilt trips? The creative alternatives are as numerous as you want them to be.

I love missions conferences and I believe they are a must for a healthy church. You try it. Make your "Opening Day" a winner and you'll have a great season!

True Grit

Talent and education don't necessarily add up to cross-cultural success. I've seen a lot of talented and highly trained missionaries bite the dust and leave the field. But one quality I've spotted in the best missionaries I know is something called "true grit"—that ability to hang in there when you feel like quitting.

When I want to remind myself what that sterling quality looks like, I turn towards baseball, and specifically to Luis Tiant and game four of the 1975 World Series. The lowly Boston Red Sox faced the unbeatable Cincinnati Reds, whose roster contained some of the greatest names in modern baseball: Johnny Bench, Joe Morgan, Tony Perez, and Pete Rose.

In game one, Red Sox pitcher Luis Tiant was dazzling, and they beat the Reds 6-0. Cincinnati came back to win games two and three, so game four became critical if Boston was to keep its hopes alive. When Tiant took the mound in game four, his arm was dead. By the fourth inning they were barely ahead of Cincinnati, 4-5. Could Tiant hold that slender lead for five long innings? He held on until in the bottom of the ninth, with runners on base and two outs, he faced the deadly Joe Morgan. On his 168th straight pitch, Tiant got Morgan to pop out to end the game. It was one of the greatest pitching performances people had ever seen, for Luis Tiant had pitched on heart alone.

When I need to reach down a little deeper in facing a tough challenge, I look at the baseball that sits on my desk in a round plastic case. It contains the faded blue signature of Luis Tiant, and it works better than the training books.

—*Mark Shaw, teacher at Nairobi Evangelical Graduate School of Theology with AIM in Kenya*

5
Keeping Players Healthy

Ways to Care for Returning Missionaries

"It's impossible to build relationships with missionaries when they arrive in town as 'professional Christians,' do their dog and pony show, and then move on."

The 1956 World Series will probably always be remembered for the unforgettable play at home plate. The Brooklyn Dodgers were playing the New York Yankees. It was the last World Series for Jackie Robinson. In the first game, Jackie had hit a single, a double, and a triple. On the memorable play at home plate, Jackie had started out on third base, taking off on the pitch to slide home. Yogi Berra was catching for the Yankees at the time, and he thought he had Jackie out, but the umpire called him safe! It was the most exciting and controversial play of the game. The fans went crazy, and the Dodgers went on to win.

I'm convinced that for returning missionaries the "play at

home" can be one of the most important, controversial, and difficult times in their career. Some are safe at home, but the truth is, some get thrown out. How does that happen?

> **Missionaries often dread the year at home. I call it "death by deputation."**

I talk to missionaries and they often dread the year at home. I call it "death by deputation." If you have fifty churches and individuals to see and fifty-two Sundays at home—think about it. It's exhausting, especially with small children. You have to be on your best behavior, and you often don't have more than a day with each group of people. How can any of us expect to have any kind of real, honest, growing relationship with people who are with us for a Sunday once every four years?

What can the church do to keep our missionaries healthy? How can we help and not hurt them at "home plate"?

I think the best way to get at this whole topic is to use a list of ideas that ACMC developed after interviewing and questioning a lot of missionaries. I have been able to spend a lot of time talking with both missionaries and supporting churches, so I hear both sides. This list really covers what's important. First, let's look at what missionaries don't like, and then we'll talk about what they love.

Missionaries do not want to be put on a pedestal.

You can't develop close relationships when people put you in a special category as though you are, or should be, super spiritual and able to handle any problem. This actually closes down communication, because missionaries burdened with such expectations fear telling anyone when they need help or can't cope.

It is also impossible to develop friendships and build relationships when you arrive in town as a "professional Christian," are expected to do your "dog and pony show" and move on. Much of the reason I decided not to take a job in the minor leagues as an umpire was because I saw the dangers of the lifestyle umpires and ball players lived. They would come into town, play their game, stay at a motel, and move on. It was incredibly destructive to marriages and families. Are we expecting the same from our missionaries?

I have two suggestions for the problem of putting missionaries on pedestals:

1. *Reduce the number of churches a person needs to see.* The local church needs to handle this one. When a couple comes to you in Atlanta, and the closest supporting church they have is in Wyoming, then you have to say, "We believe in what you're doing, but your closest church is in Wyoming. It would be unfair to you for us to support you." Taking them on would mean asking them for enormous commitments of travel time and money, and that's not good stewardship. (If a wife is from California and has family there, and the husband is from Maine, that's another story.)

I'm so encouraged that some evangelical churches and agencies are starting to work together on this. Black Rock Congregational Church in Connecticut is one example. They are part of a cooperative effort among area churches that have similar missions policies and goals, to support the same missionaries within their area. As they work together to provide financial backing, they often take on fewer missionaries for larger amounts. This keeps the missionaries around longer and the people can get to know them as real people. They come down from the pedestal.

2. *Help missionaries develop effective presentations with honesty*

and genuine openness. Sometimes missionaries should be asked to talk about anything but missions. They need to let their hair down, be authentic. Missionaries have other interests apart from missions. Do you know much about your missionaries apart from their mission work?

I had a young couple come and ask me to critique their missions presentation when they were just beginning to speak in churches. The husband was a brilliant guy, but dry as dust. His wife, on the other hand, has an effective presence and is an excellent communicator. After the presentation I sat down with them and said, "Do you want me to tell the truth?" They said okay. So I said to the husband, "You take about two minutes to speak at the end; otherwise let your wife do the presentation—she's terrific."

> *Missionaries are not replacements for the pastor. They need a pastor. Don't let your pastor leave town when the missionaries arrive.*

I went with them to their next two churches, and she wowed them. Both churches took on their support. She knew what to say in a natural way, and she understood people. While he could be deadly, she could represent them as real, regular people. This couple made themselves accountable to me for their presentations. I talked to a pastor of a church in New Jersey that took on some of their support. He said to me, "The people really loved them. The wife is great. He's kind of an intellectual." I bit my tongue.

Missionaries do not want to be pastor replacements.

Missionaries need pastors. They are not replacements for the pastor. The don't want to be used as pulpit supply when the pastor is on vacation. They need to see that the pastor supports them, and that he is there to listen to them. The pastor should be pastoring the missionaries in your church.

One of our best friends is a woman whose nine-year-old son was crushed to death in an accident in Africa. I remember praying for that woman. She was back on home assignment one year after the accident and told Nancy and me the story of how she was wrestling with God. She wanted to quit missions and quit being a Christian. She wondered how she could continue if God was a God who would take away her son while she was serving him.

When we asked her how she made it through this experience, she told us the story of how her pastor in Oregon phoned her in Africa every day for six days to talk to her and listen to her. And then she said, "After the phone calls stopped, the letters came." And she showed Nancy and me the letters; she still carried them in her purse.

Now that man was pastoring his missionaries. He was there for her. Statistics say that 40 percent of the missionaries returning home need some kind of counseling. Don't let your pastor leave town when the missionaries arrive. They need a pastor.

Missionaries do not want to be asked to give a one-minute report in twenty-five words or less.
Would you like to have to stand up and tell people in one minute what you had poured your life into for the past four years? What would you say? What would your pastor say if he was asked to give a one-minute report on his ministry for the past four years?

Of course, I want to emphasize again that you must use your missionaries' time and gifts properly. If your missionary is not a good speaker, don't put him or her in the pulpit. So, how do you highlight a missionary if not in the pulpit? One of the best missionaries I know does his best sharing when he's working with other people engineering a water project or roofing a church. He's a perfect candidate for the "Home Improvement" men's breakfast.

Another missionary I know told a men's group how he loved to hunt in Tanzania. These guys took him deer hunting and on the first day he had caught the limit for every guy in the group. They were all angry because they had to come home after the first day, but after that, they listened to this guy when he talked. I remember when he was leaving to go back to Africa, all he had for his carry-on luggage were his two prized guns. He was a man's man and had his particular crowd. You need to help your missionaries find their crowd.

Missionaries do not want to come home and find that no one is prepared to welcome them.

The children especially hate finding the old family picture on the missions display while the new one gathers dust on a shelf somewhere. If Susie is now a lovely seventeen-year-old and you've displayed her thirteen-year-old picture with braces and pigtails, she'll not be pleased.

It also hurts when the pastor announces the Smiths and their three lovely children and it's clear he doesn't know the names of those three children. Missionaries tell me that they are sometimes introduced as working in a country they have never even visited. One missionary woman told me her son wondered as they arrived at churches, "Well, does anybody want to bet whether the pastor at this church will get it right?"

You can solve these kinds of problems by keeping the names and ministries before the people continuously—not just at missions conferences. Give out bookmarks one month with all the names of the missionaries on them. At a church dinner have place mats with the missionaries and mission fields on them. Have somebody who's creative invent a board game to educate the church regarding the missionaries and their fields, and then sell the games to the church families or give them to the Sunday school classes.

Missionaries do not want their prayer letters to be ignored.

Nothing hurts like finding your prayer letters edited beyond recognition or piled in a corner table in the church basement with the old issues of *Decision* magazines. Baseball cards improve with age, but not prayer letters.

One thing our missions committee did was make what became known as "The Red Book." I realized our people didn't know our missionaries, so we prepared one of these books for each family in the church. It was a three-ring notebook, with a page for each missionary family giving their photo, birthdays, mission field, job description, favorite foods—lots of things. I visited many homes where these books were on the dining room table so the family could pray through them regularly. What a difference it makes to people who have been gone for so long to know they are remembered.

Missionaries do not want to be objects of curiosity.

One missionary woman said to me, "People don't ask me how I'm coping, or what my concerns are. They say, 'What do you eat? Any snake stories?'" Missionaries love to discuss the cultures they live in, but their work and relationships and hardships need to be taken seriously too.

A helpful book for people who want to treat missionaries right is *Serving as Senders* by Neal Pirolo. It's filled with practical ideas to help the local church be the support team that missionaries need when they come home.

What are some of the positive ways congregations can care for returning missionaries?

Missionaries are very grateful for the many things that people in their local churches have done. So here's the good news and some proven ways congregations can help.

Welcome missionaries into your homes and treat them as beloved guests.

This often benefits the church even more than the missionary. In the first church where I was missions chairman, we used to bring in thirty-five missionaries the week of the conference and put them all in homes. One of the results of that became known just a couple of years ago when I was teaching at Columbia International University.

> *I'm doing what I'm doing today partly because my parents always seemed to have our house full of missionaries.*

After class a young man came up to me and introduced himself. I realized I knew the family so we got to talking and he told me he was studying to go to the mission field. I asked him how that decision came about and he explained.

During one of the missions conferences you used to run when I was a little boy, you put a missionary in our home named Nan Grey. She used to get down on the floor with me when I was little and play with me. My mother and father would often go out, and she'd put me to bed and pray with me. She wrote me letters from the mission field when she went away. She sent me Christmas cards and birthday cards. And every time she came home, she'd stay at our house. God used her in my life and I believe that is why I'm studying here today.

About a year and a half ago a missionary friend called me one evening. She and her husband have six children. They were going to be in our area the next weekend and one of their engagements had been canceled. She asked if I could find them a place to stay and use them at church that weekend. I said, "Sure," and went through our entire church directory (which has 700 entries). But nobody would host a family with six kids. I called a family back who had three kids of their own. After a bit of pleading on my part, Mrs. Armstrong said she'd take them for the weekend.

When I hung up, my wife said, "You have just made an enemy, putting six kids in with someone who has three kids. They'll tear the house apart."

The weekend went by and I didn't hear much. On Monday night as I was sitting down to watch a baseball game, my wife handed me the phone and said, "Just desserts. It's Mrs. Armstrong."

What I heard on the phone were these words, "Tom, I just want to thank you for the gift of a wonderful weekend. That family sat down with us and we had devotions together. Our kids learned from their kids. It was a highlight of the year for us."

I'm doing what I'm doing today partly because my parents always seemed to have our house full of missionaries. We took the families with loads of kids that no one else could take. My parents treated missionaries like honored guests. I remember once my dad stopped at a meat store on the way home from a meeting and bought steaks and sausages. I was thrilled. Then, before we got home he stopped off at an apartment where some missionaries were staying and gave them the steaks. We drove on with the sausages. Tell me that didn't speak volumes to me as a kid who happened to like steak a lot!

One time I was at a missions conference as it was closing and people were giving their testimonies. One old guy stood up and said, "I never liked missions. I never knew any of these people. I didn't know what to say to them. Well, a couple of years ago I was asked to take care of a missionary and take him to a ball game. I rode the bus to the game with him and we talked during the game and we rode back together. I've been writing him ever since."

There's a man in our church who takes missionary families out for dinner when they first come home and then he says, "Here's my credit card, everybody gets a new outfit on me." He has been blessed with a financial position that allows him to do that kind of thing, and it means so much to the missionary families. I remember one mother telling me she had dressed the kids all in the best outfits they had for their arrival back in the States. She thought they all looked pretty good. But when they were met at the airport, suddenly everything they had on looked dull and shabby. Can you imagine what those new outfits mean?

I can't say enough about missionary hospitality and the impact it can have on the life of your congregation.

Treat missionaries as regular people.

One night of a missions conference, have all the missionaries tell what their hobbies are and demonstrate them if possible. I was at a church once where a church planter in Paris was visiting. He was also a jazz pianist, and that night the missionaries were demonstrating their hobbies. This guy went up, lifted up the top of that grand piano, and played jazz for about ten minutes. He changed the image of missions for those people.

Write letters and send care packages to missionaries.

Do you realize that missionaries get very little mail? Sometimes the only mail they get from your church is an annual questionnaire with hard questions that the resident members would never have to answer. Send a postcard or a brief note. Get a list of your missionaries' E-mail addresses on the Internet, and zip off a few sentences of encouragement or news.

I've had the job of writing to our missionaries twice a year on behalf of the congregation, and I write to some of them personally. One time I asked each of them to send me a letter telling how many letters of encouragement they had gotten in the previous six months. Some had received one or two, some had received none. I made up a brochure for the church giving the addresses of all of our missionaries and suggestions of what to write to a missionary. Some people ask, "You mean a missionary would want to hear from me?" Absolutely! In the brochure I also included a tear-jerking poem about a missionary going to the mailbox and finding nothing there.

The next week I did another sneaky thing. I got about 100 airforms, addressed them to missionaries, and taped them under the pews before church. I didn't tell anybody this. On Sunday morning I got up and said, "How many of you people love our missionaries?" Everybody raised their hands. Then I said, "How many of you are willing to write to our missionaries?" About 400 raised their hands. Then I said, "Keep your hand out and reach it all the way down and under your pew. Some of you will find an airform under there all addressed, stamped, and ready to go."

Do you know what happened after that letter-writing campaign? People wrote and they got letters back. If we got ten or fifteen people interested in a missionary from that one experience, it was worth it all.

A woman I know who lives in Tanzania has four children.

She was asked what small thing the church could do for her family that was not too expensive. She said, "My kids love Kool-Aid and with four thirsty kids, there's never enough. So when you write, please enclose a package of Kool-Aid." A few months later she wrote me and said, "Tom, you'll never guess, but to date I've received 586 packets of Kool-Aid!"

Send cassette tapes, videos, good magazines—sports, homemaking, fashion—and clippings from the hometown newspaper. There's no end to small things that can be a great encouragement to missionaries. Remember that many foreign countries charge large customs fees to pick up a package. So check with the mission agency about procedures before sending large stuff.

Meet with individual missionaries to discuss his or her ministry, goals, or personal problems.

Sometimes missionaries need a place to talk about the victories and the losses, about their future dreams for their work. They need a chance to unload. They can't get into all this on Sunday, or at a large meeting. They need the ear of a supportive missions committee, and the committee needs to make this happen.

Help missionaries continue their education.

Missionaries love having an opportunity to take courses. They need to retool and find out what is going on in their field just like the rest of us. Some churches have missionaries serve on staff while continuing their education. If your church can help make that happen, everyone benefits—the missionary, the people they minister to, and you.

Give missionaries a vacation.

When asked what churches do for them that really helps, one missionary couple said they have a supporting church that sends them to a nice resort for a few days before they begin their home assignment. The church says, "You need a break to get your act together and rest. This is our gift to you." The missionaries said, "That tells us they love us. We do need time after reentry to get our act together."

Show missionaries you care about their children.

What about a scholarship for an MK? What about inviting college-age missionary kids to your house for Thanksgiving or Christmas if they have no family around? What about helping them find a summer job, or offering them one if you have a business that hires summer help? What about teaching them to drive? Some kids can't get their licenses in the country where their parents serve. What about writing to the kids who go to boarding schools? What about taking an MK shopping on Christmas break?

Send people to visit missionaries and help them on the job.

Many people have the funds to take a trip and see a missionary, or even visit a missionary as part of their vacation. As I've said before, nothing compares to this kind of experience for raising people's interest, awareness, commitment, and passion. I know a successful electrical contractor who went with a team to Guatemala to work on a building project there. This guy Ken was one of those people who was always negative about missions. He even told me I was "ripping off the church" with all this missions stuff. But, after we sent him to Guatemala to do electrical work and stay with some missionaries, he became one of the biggest backers of missions in his church. He had seen what those missionaries were doing, and he had put in 18-hour days right along with them. Later he went back on his own to help them get the job done, and today he and his wife are on the mission field as short-term workers in Kenya.

Have a missions "pro."

Every church needs someone who understands and cares for missionaries beyond just serving on the missions committee or doing a missions task in the church. A missions pro is a unique person with missions in his or her heart. I meet these special people in churches wherever I travel.

In my home church, the missions pro was a woman named Jean McKinley. She modeled a missions heart. We went to Jean when I needed to know something about a missionary. She understood reentry stress and knew just what missionaries needed. She decorated missionarys' apartments and refused any donation that wouldn't meet the standards of any regular church member—no attic stuff was allowed. She and her husband would put up any missionary at any time, last minute or not. They'd pick people up at the airport. They planned dinners for missionaries. They knew who liked coffee and who liked pistachio ice cream. Jean knew the missionary kids' birthdays and sent them cards. She knew just what a retired missionary would like to do for an outing or when he or she might need a phone call.

> *Every church needs a "missions pro" who understands and cares for missionaries beyond just serving on the missions committee.*

This is not a job you can sign up for. I see it as a gift and a calling. But missionaries love to know these people. They seem to be the very people God puts in churches to make it "safe at home."

The church at home can play a big role in making their missionaries more effective and able to return to their cross-cultural ministries with renewed energy. Take the initiative in taking care of your "players" and giving them a safe place to call home.

The Hallowed Hall

If you call yourself a baseball fan and have never been to Cooperstown, New York, your life is not complete. There are two times in your life you should go to the Hall of Fame: when you are very young (and you wish you were older) and when you are much older (and you wish you were younger). I have done both.

The first time I went to Cooperstown I was nine years old. The M & M Boys ruled New York, Willie Mays was hitting everything in sight, the bum Dodgers (now out in Los Angeles) had a couple of pitchers named Koufax and Drysdale, and the Cubs were in last place. I had never seen a place so majestic, so hallowed . . . and I had grown up going to church.

On that visit I was able to stick my pinky finger through the hole of Babe Ruth's locker and touch his original uniform! The glow lasted long enough to return home and show my friends. I remember, too, that I had a big argument with my dad. He wanted to buy me a book on baseball and I wanted one of the miniature souvenir wooden baseball bats. Dad was trying to herd five kids through the Hall of Fame that day and really didn't have the time for an argument. He gave me an ultimatum: the book or nothing. I took the book.

In 1995 I went back to Cooperstown with my own kids. It hadn't changed much in thirty-five years. The building didn't look as big, and Doubleday

Field looked like a Little League park. I walked through with my kids noting the heroes of the past. We stopped at Babe Ruth's locker and I stared at the locker and the very small holes of the grating. I couldn't imagine getting my finger through there to touch the uniform.

It was a different perspective on the Hall of Fame. Still inspiring, still majestic, and just as pastoral as in years past. The desire to tie on sneakers and run hard to the outfield still rushed across me. It was the nine-year-old boy who had changed. Except, on the way out I purchased a small, wooden bat at the gift shop.

—*Rick Mead, Director of Vietnamese/Filipino Ministry with International Teams, Philadelphia*

6

The Big Leagues

The Top Ten Mistakes Mission Agencies Make

"Mission agencies are not 'the other guys.' We are on the same team. I owe much to missions executives who kept me in the game when I wanted to throw down my glove and get out."

In 1994, John Orme, who was then the head of the IFMA, a fellowship of mission agencies, asked me to address a gathering of missions organizations on the top mistakes mission agencies make. I had spoken on this topic in other contexts, but this would be to a group of people whose accumulated wisdom was awe-inspiring to me. The group included Ralph Winter, president of the U. S. Center for World Mission, Ted Barnett, General Director of AIM International, and Jim Plueddemann, General Director of SIM. It was staggering. Before the meeting I was up most of the night pacing and praying. I'm known for my outspokenness, so I felt like the George Steinbrenner of missions. I thought I might lose some friends by speaking my mind to these folks.

Incredibly, the last time I had been in the same hotel in

Charlotte, North Carolina, I had been speaking to a gathering of the NCAA and ECAC baseball umpires on "How to Deal with Ejections." I always try to teach an umpire to stay away from trouble because there's enough trouble anyway. You are wrong 50 percent of the time when you umpire a baseball game. When you call a third strike on a guy, you don't walk toward his dugout; you head the other way. So what was I doing at this meeting, walking right into the "other team's" dugout?

I need to say up front that many leaders of mission agencies have had a big influence on my life. They are not "the other guys." We are on the same team. I owe so much to missions executives who kept me in the game when I wanted to throw down my glove and get out. The Christian life is not a solitary journey. It is a pilgrimage made in the company of the committed. I know that when I am in the company of missions leaders I am with committed people.

> *I hope that I upset and bother people, because change is needed if we are to stay effective.*

I believe in mission agencies, but I also believe that we need some changes. We need to do things differently because the church in North America has changed. I know change is difficult. My wife does a lot of baby-sitting, and I think the only person who likes change is a baby with a wet diaper. I hope that I upset and bother people, because change is needed if we are to stay effective.

How did you come up with these Top Ten Mistakes?

After I started guest lecturing at Columbia International

University, I realized that my course made suggestions and offered critiques on agencies and church relations. John Orme heard what I was teaching and then asked me to do my lecture for the mission agency people who needed to hear it the most. I decided I'd better do some serious checking and research to make sure I was right.

My research method was just to ask questions and keep asking questions. I asked missions chairpersons; I asked pastors; I asked church workers; I asked missions leaders everywhere I went for a six-month period: "What do you think of the agencies? How do you get along with agencies? Do you have any problems with agencies? Tell me now because in a few months I'll be your voice in front of their CEOs." I had some volunteers in my office call missions chairpersons for me and do surveys with these same questions. Finally, I focused my findings into the ten mistakes discussed below.

Mistake #1: Agencies often do not communicate well with the sending churches about personnel changes.

I sat down with a leading missions pastors for breakfast one morning, and this was the first thing he said: "Nothing is more disturbing to us than when we have a candidate with an agency and the next thing we know he has changed fields or changed countries or been called home to work in the home office, and we were never told anything about it. It is very upsetting. People don't like those kinds of surprises."

Agencies need to take the time to communicate with people.

Mistake #2: Agencies are often reluctant to deal with incompetence.

During my years as a missions chairman, our church had a case that we just couldn't wrestle with ourselves. We realized that one of our missionaries was not competent to do the particular job he had been assigned to do. We needed the agency, but it wasn't there for us. So the church flew me to the field, and I pleaded with the missionary: "Let us bring you home where you can get a job where you will feel more fulfilled. We'll help." Unfortunately, with no support from that agency, our efforts were not successful, and the guy is still on the field today. Nobody wants to deal with incompetence. Maybe we think it isn't spiritual.

Another time, I sat in a motel room in Atlanta talking with a man I supervised with ACMC whom I had to let go. He loved the Lord, and he had raised a percentage of his support, but he just wasn't cutting it. It wasn't easy. I sat and cried, and his wife accused me of not discipling him and helping him make it.

A friend recently reminded me that when he and I were working together we had urged the church to take on a young couple. But later we saw problems, and we both agreed that it was time to bring the couple home and get them a job in the States. The agency did not want to go through that experience, so, in the last ten years our church and others have given that couple $300,000 of the Lord's money. When we give money, it's not our money. When it goes down a dark hole, we're wasting the Lord's money.

I've heard about these kinds of problems from missions executives as well. One director told me, "I was just called home from the field, and I'm now running this agency. I have 300 missionaries and probably about 100 of them I should let go." I listen to missions specialists Ted Ward and Phil Parshall who suggest that 40 percent of the missionary force is ineffective. I pray that they're wrong, but what if they're right?

As we see some changes in churches with young business executives coming onto missions committees and expecting standards and accountability, I'm getting questions I never got before. Are we going to wrestle with this hard stuff? It's difficult.

In Acts 13, the church prayed and worshiped and then carefully chose a select few to go. There were many who were willing, but the church needed to discern whom God would send.

Agencies need a good way to evaluate their personnel. One way to determine whether an agency is taking that part of the job seriously is to call and ask them how many people they turn down.

In baseball you get cut or sent down to the minors if you aren't working out. Maybe we need to send some of our people down to the minors or to a different league to get more training or experience when they need it. Branch Rickey, who was the manager of the St. Louis Cardinals in the 1920s, started the idea of the farm teams. You had to prove yourself on the farm teams before you were brought up to the major leagues. That's not a bad model for training missionary personnel.

> *In baseball, you have to prove yourself on the farm teams before you are brought up to the major leagues. That's not a bad model for training missionary personnel.*

Mistake #3: The agency's board of directors may not represent the actual constituency of supporting churches.

Most boards of mission agencies are not typical of the people who support the agency. Age is a factor for example. Many board members who are in their sixties and seventies cannot easily relate to today's boomers and busters culture. More baby-boomers are moving into leadership in our churches each year, yet most mission agencies have very few boomers on their boards. They must be allowed to give of their time and talents to the organization. It is not true that the board's only purpose is to raise money. It also needs to represent the constituency of its supporters.

Agency board members need to be sold out for missions. How can they make the significant decisions they need to make if they are not both passionate and informed about the current missions scene? When I was on the staff of ACMC, once in a while I would ask the director if I could address the board, when they met just before the ACMC National Conference. What bothered me most was that five of the board members went home before the conference even began! I know these are busy people, but are they really committed to what the mission is doing?

Mistake #4: Agencies often allow no input from supporting churches regarding agency strategies.

I asked someone to do a telephone survey of mission agencies to gather information. One of the questions I had her ask was this: "We have a group of people that we have trained and prepared to go to X country. Could we do it through your agency?" Seventy percent said they wouldn't touch that opportunity with a ten-foot pole.

Right now in my office I have two letters from excellent churches that have put teams together. They want to find an agency that will handle the team, but they are having trouble. In reality this is the trend—churches putting teams together and training them—and agencies will have to adapt to this change in strategy. Churches are becoming proactive. They want more input, and they are ready to make the commitment of people and finances. Agencies must not close the door on them.

Mistake #5: Agencies do not have a clear vision statement.

If you talk to me very long, you will see that I am big on vision and developing meaningful vision statements. It's true, even in missions, that "where there is no vision the people perish" (Proverbs 29:18, KJV).

There are a lot of people on missions committees who know very little, and when they listen to missionary visitors, they want to hear a clear statement of the agency's vision and of the missionary's place in that vision. Every agency needs a short, succinct, understandable mission statement that every missionary knows. CAM International has just re-vamped their vision statement and a number of other agencies are beginning to wrestle with this task.

ACMC recently hired a woman to do fundraising, and she impressed me in a meeting with their staff when she got up, lit a match, and before the match burned out she told us ACMC's purpose statement. It said something to all of us. Can the agency people tell others the vision of the agency? Can the board members

> *Mission agencies need a clear purpose statement. If they can't tell it to you in a minute, forget it.*

do that? Can the home office personnel? If we don't have a clear vision, maybe we're redundant and we aren't even aware of it. I tell people who are looking for an agency to ask prospective ones to give their vision or purpose. If they can't tell it to you in a minute, forget it.

Mistake #6: Agencies often do not cooperate with one another.

I once showed a businessman friend a handbook that lists

every known mission agency (put out by MARC, the Missions Advanced Research and Communication Center). "Why are there so many agencies? Why is there so much duplication?" he wondered. I agreed that more cooperation between agencies needs to be encouraged.

Then I showed him some ways this is beginning to happen. The Co-Mission Program is an attempt to get mission agencies to cooperate on certain mission initiatives. The Alliance for Saturation Church Planting is another inter-mission, cooperative effort. Agencies cooperate to plant churches in target countries. We must see more of this cooperation.

Are agencies willing to cooperate with one another and work with one another? I think that's one of the pressing problems with mission agencies. Too many of them are not aggressively seeking to work together. When missionaries are working together out on the field, they don't care what a colleague's denominational or agency affiliation is, as long as he or she can get the job done. Eight thousand miles away from home, it just doesn't matter that much.

At one ACMC national conference, Ron Cline, the president of HCJB, told how the three largest missionary radio networks in the world, Trans World Radio, HCJB, and FEBC, got together. Instead of reaching into the same countries, they realized that all the duplication was crazy. They looked at their transmitting areas, cut the pie up into three slices, and are using their resources to reach even more countries together. There is great wisdom in approaching the work of missions that way.

Mistake #7: Agency home offices are often poorly managed.

When I came home from my first ACMC conference, it occurred to me that we hadn't given any of our missionaries a raise in the previous ten years. This really bothered me. So

I raised the money to give every one of our missionaries a raise. Al Larsen, who was director of the Unevangelized Fields Mission (UFM), told me the rate of inflation in all the countries where our missionaries served. UFM's financial man crunched the numbers for me and we figured out how we could pay the raises. Then I wrote to all the agencies, asking them what the support figures should be for the next year and waited for replies.

You know what? I only got a 70 percent reply. And these were agencies we were sending money to! Now I know you can blame some things on the mail, but not everything. A big missions supporter recently told me he wondered if mission agencies had their offices on auto pilot. Perhaps I sound harsh, but think about it. Churches are giving the agencies their sons and daughters and God's money, and sometimes they can't even get the right person to handle a serious question or answer mail. No agency should hide behind the excuse that it's a faith-run missions organization. There is no reason to be shoddy. None of us is perfect and I can be guilty of some of the things I am talking about. All of us must work toward better handling of the resources and responsibilities we have.

Mistake #8: Agencies encourage missionaries to raise support from individuals outside of their local churches.

I am a churchman. I love the church. Anyone who hears me speak knows I am biased toward the local church. So this mistake scares and troubles me, because it reduces the role of the local church in missions.

Recently I asked some mission agencies what percentage of their funds comes from individuals and what percentage comes from churches. The average was about 70 percent from individuals and 30 percent from churches. Then I asked, "Can you give me the figures for twenty years ago?" The average back then was just the opposite, 70 percent from churches and 30 percent from individuals. I know I need to address the condition of the church today and the reality of the giving patterns of the baby boomers and busters. That's a separate concern. But it bothers me that I see this imbalance in fundraising.

Do you know what bothers me even more? Mission agencies in their candidate schools (and I teach in some of them) spend six hours teaching their candidates how to raise money from individuals and half an hour teaching them to raise money from the church. Sure, it's harder to get money from the church, but unless this trend stops, the local church will be helpless in the missions endeavor. How can we have any accountability if missionaries turn their backs on the sending church and raise money from friends?

Isn't the goal of missions to plant churches that will reproduce churches? If this trend keeps developing, the church won't even be in the picture. I have trouble with this one biblically. God has called the church to send out people. Agencies can change this trend, and some of them are working on it. I was thrilled to hear this from the woman I spoke to at one agency: "We spend 90 percent of our time telling people to raise their money from the church." Sure, it's going to take a little longer, but I'm convinced it's the way to go.

Mistake #9: Agencies are not addressing the growing perception that support figures are unjustifiably high.

We discussed before our need to encourage giving in congregations, but we have to look at the other side of the question as well. In our economy, many people are taking pay cuts or facing unemployment, yet they continue to tithe faithfully.

This adds even more weight to the argument for accountability and cost-effectiveness at mission agencies.

I have missionary friends who complain that their support figures are too high and this is often due to agency costs. I went to a mission agency to help a missionary who was supported by my home church. He had raised $50,000 and he needed $62,000. I said to the agency, "I'm here on behalf of this missionary; he's been trained and he spent three years in ministry in our church. We believe he is well-qualified and needs to go. There are three things in this budget figure that he can do without." I asked them to eliminate those items. And they did.

> *We have to go back to the basics and teach people why we do missions. How much time do agencies spend helping churches understand why they do missions?*

I think missions committes and mission agencies need to take a hard look at the costs. Recently I received a letter from a church with one missionary's support figure of $86,000. Business people on that committee are wrestling with high figures like that. I'm not against high figures—in some cases we need to defend them; but we had better have a good reason for them. Low figures are not necessarily more virtuous either.

I used to be a basher of the mission agencies when it came to finances. But the church makes lots of mistakes as well when it comes to missionary support. Let's help each other. As a pastor friend of mine said, "One day I will be accountable for how every dollar of this church's money was spent."

Mistake #10: Agencies apply too little effort helping churches build a missions vision.

A pastor phoned me about coming to his church to speak. I asked him about his experience with mission agencies, and what he said cut me to the heart: "I've been a pastor for over twenty years and I have never once had anyone from a missions agency call and offer me help."

Jim Plueddemann, General Director of SIM, said in an interview, "Instead of just harvesting trees, we need to plant trees." I agree wholeheartedly. Unless agencies go back to helping churches and spending time building relationships, we're in trouble. Biblically, I know that God is going to get the job done. My question is, Is he going to bypass agencies to do so?

The church in America needs direction and vision in missions. We have to go back to the basics and teach people why we do missions. How much time do agencies spend helping churches understand why they do missions? We need teaching and leading agencies, caring and relationship-building agencies. If agencies do that job first, their needs will be met.

How can agencies get personal and be helpful to every local church? How can they share vision and give specific assistance?

I have come down very hard on agencies in my list of mistakes, but I see all kinds of reasons for hope. I see a great future for churches and agencies working together. Here are some of my ideas.

Agencies can care about the local church.

When I first went into missions motivation, I decided that one day a week I would drive to a church that was within a two-hour drive of my office, visit the pastor, and tell him I was there to encourage and pray for him. I'd ask him to give me a couple of things I could pray about. At the first church I went to, the pastor said, "Well, I don't have a lot of time." I said, "Just give me two minutes. How can I pray for you? I want to put you on my prayer list." He wasn't overjoyed, but he did give me one or two things to pray about. Recently I looked at my church support list and I realized that almost all the churches that support me began with that kind of a relationship.

If agencies are concerned about the church in America, the church where they get their candidates and their money, then I think they need to take a big interest in the local churches. Agencies need to go to churches as helpers and encouragers, not just as recruiters and solicitors. They need to know which churches have missions pastors and which ones have volunteer chairpersons. They have to spend time learning about the churches so they can offer the right kind of help.

Agencies can become missionaries to the church in North America.

This means taking the time to get to know the culture in America. It also means keeping up with the changes in our culture, just the way they expect their missionaries to know the cultures where they serve. I love the expression, "When the horse dies, dismount." I hope none of our agencies are sitting on dead horses. Agency personnel might benefit from a helpful new management book called *Managing at the Speed of Change* by Daryl Conner. In a changing time for churches, agencies need to be there to guide them through the developing scene in missions.

Agencies can also help churches by spending more time with them. This may mean recognizing that agencies are actually assisting the local church in doing the work that God has given it to do, rather than thinking they are getting the church to support their work.

Agencies can help local churches develop their own missions vision and not force them to accept a prepackaged vision of their agency.

Agencies need to keep the bigger picture more firmly in mind. I overheard one missions representative talking with a young women interested in missions. He explained to her what his agency was all about, and she told him what her gifts and desires were. Then he said, "You really don't fit our agency, but let me help you find the one that you should go with." Isn't that great? Rather than recruiting just for the sake of recruiting, he helped that woman develop her own gifts and find where they could be used best. Unfortunately, this kind of attitude is not as common as it should be. Are we in competition with one another?

> *Mission reps often forget to contextualize their language. You can't speak "missionese" from the pulpit.*

I get about thirty-five calls a week from churches, and one-third of them are from new missions committee people who say they don't know what they are doing and need help. I'd like to be able to say to these people, "So and so at X mission agency lives near you, and he'll come over and help you develop a vision for your church." But I haven't found a lot of agencies that want to do that and not carry their baggage with them.

Agencies can do their best to find positive representatives who understand their culture.

I'm ashamed to say that the criticisms I hear most frequently are about agency representatives and what they do. Reps too often forget to contextualize their language so today's people will hear what they say. You can't speak "missionese" from the pulpit. If you stand up and say SIM, IFMA, AIM, and UFM, many young people won't even know what you're talking about.

I spoke at a baby-boomer church recently and one of the men on the platform who knew me quite well said, "Tom, no figures and no initials." Learn how to communicate so people can hear the challenge.

Agencies can get back to the basics.

We can't assume that people today believe that lost people will go to hell. I was shocked recently when Frank Severn of Send International asked a group of college students, "How many of you people believe lost people go to hell?" This was a good Bible college, and he was speaking to the freshman class. Only about 80 percent of them believed that lost people go to hell. Those students are going to have trouble with missions.

I'm sorry, but if you don't believe sinners are going to hell, then why in the world do missions?

I'm finding more and more churches backing off the truth that sinners are going to hell. Well, I'm sorry, but if you don't believe sinners are going to hell, then why in the world do missions? We need to go back and teach the biblical basis of missions, plain and simple. Work it in to every message. We can't assume Christians understand.

When I look back on it, I'm still amazed at the warm response I received when I presented these things to the group of mission agency leaders. I did have to defend some of my controversial points in the "post-game show." But one missions leader gave me a big hug and said, "We all needed to hear this. Don't back down on anything." Now that keeps a guy in the game.

Baseball and Grace

Growing up in a church that condemned just about everything a young person wanted to do, I was always on the prowl for small glimpses of grace. One such glimpse appeared to me on the day of the big game when the West Side played North Street in the annual sandlot classic.

I belonged to the West Side, a blue-collar, racially integrated neighborhood. North Street was the proper side of town. People who lived on the West Side went to the shoe factory. People who lived on North Street went to Harvard. The annual baseball game between these two sides of town was as much about democracy and dignity as it was about baseball.

The trouble with this year's game was that it came on a Sunday, a day on which *no* sports should be played, according to my parents and my church. I was just going to watch, I promised my parents. Reluctantly they gave me permission to go and watch. When I arrived, my West Side teammates were one man short. They knew about my Sunday scruples but asked me to play anyway.

Now, when one believes that the whole American way of life is at stake and that somehow a single baseball game will decide our fate as a nation, it is easy to rationalize doing just about anything. It was in this frame of mind that I brought the matter before God in a quick prayer. (I did most of the talking.) I asked for grace—a little unmerited favor. I didn't really expect that I'd get it. Then I borrowed a glove and trotted out to right field.

In the bottom of the eighth inning, our team was behind by a run with two men on base, and I was up at bat. I hadn't done much in my previous at bats. Easy fly ball outs. My impotence at the plate was justice, I figured. What more could I expect for disobeying Sabbath law?

But this last time at bat something strange happened: I swung a tad late and arched a high ball deep into left field. It rolled long enough for me to get to second base and for the two runners to score. We had pulled ahead and held the lead to win! We taught those North Siders a lesson or two about equality.

But that's not the lesson I learned. I learned that sometimes we don't get what we deserve; sometimes we get much more. Not just a win or a blow for democracy, but grace—a smile from a gracious God who knows a whole lot more about mercy than many of us care to admit.

—Mark Shaw, teacher at Nairobi Evangelical Graduate School of Theology with AIM in Kenya

7
Integrating the Game

Partnering with African-American and Third-World Missions

"The church in the West was once considered the sending church, but now we are working hand-in-hand with many other nations towards the goal of world evangelization."

My Canadian friends say the first *real* World Series game was played in 1992 when the Toronto Blue Jays beat the Atlanta Braves in six games. It couldn't have been a World Series before because the Americans were the only ones playing. One nation doesn't make the world.

Baseball began as an American phenomenon, but it is played all over the world now. It recently became an official Olympic sport. We're getting international players on American teams. But it wasn't too long ago when nonwhite players were excluded from the game. As the first African American in the major leagues in 1947, Jackie Robinson was a great player and a great man, who helped break down the racial barrier in sports.

Sad to say, racial barriers in missions at that time in the 1940s and 1950s was just as shameful. Many large, well-known mission agencies would not accept African-American candidates. Their excuse? Since all-white churches would not support them, why set them up for disappointment? That's one of the same excuses the major leagues used. They claimed that fans wouldn't go to the games if there were African-American players, but Robinson and others sure proved they were wrong.

What "Jackie Robinson" stories are there in American missions history?

What we see throughout our early history is that African Americans who were called to missions started their own agencies, just like those great players, Satchel Paige, Jackie Robinson, and Cool Papa Bell, who played in the Negro leagues begun in the 1920s. Before mission agencies were fully developed and funded, black missionaries faced quite a struggle.

There are many outstanding people in African-American missions history. John Marrant was a man much like David Brainard in his early mission to the American Indians. George Leile formed the Jamaica Mission Society and may have been the first American to go overseas as a missionary.

There was a progressive African-American missionary named Lott Carey. I always call him the "other Carey." Lott Carey was saved in 1807, and he taught himself to read and preach. He bought his own freedom from slavery and went on to pastor an 800-member African Baptist Church in Richmond, Virginia. That church in Richmond started what may very well have been the first African-American mission society. Then Carey volunteered to be the first missionary sent from that mission society. He sailed to Liberia in 1821. Eight years later, while carrying on a successful ministry, he died in a fire.

As far as I know, the first single woman missionary sent from America was an African-American woman named Betsy Stockton. She believed God had called her to be a missionary, and the American mission board she applied with sent her as domestic help with another family. William Colley and William Henry Sheppard and others are part of a long list of African-American missionaries. I think the American church has amnesia about a lot of this part of missions history, and there's not much documentation. In Ruth Tucker's excellent book, *From Jerusalem to Irian Jaya,* there is not one African-American missionary profiled, an unfortunate omission.

Back when I was a kid in the 1940s and 1950s, an African-American man from the Carver Mission used to come see us. (Today this mission has headquarters in Atlanta, Georgia, and Don Canty is the director.) I remember that missionary visitor telling us about living in the South at that time as a negro, and trying to raise support to go overseas. There was a kind of "underground railroad" for African-American missionaries then. They knew which churches would welcome them and which ones had people who would invite them to stay in their homes.

Another African-American missionary who spoke to our church in the 1970s was a doctor named Dan McGrath. We gave him something towards his ministry. Later he brought a friend of his to see me, saying, "We went to school together and he's much more talented in ministry than I am. We've worked in campus ministry together. The problem is, he can't seem to raise his support because he's African-American. Do you think the church could give him the same amount they gave me?" We were able to help that time, but

I know there were many other cases in which young African-American missionaries could not get funded. The church at large still has a lot of catching up to do as far as African-American missions is concerned.

At the same time, some exciting things are happening today in missions in the African-American church. I attended an African-American missions conference at Washington Bible College in 1994. In addition, I am aware of thirteen different African-American mission agencies that are growing. There may be many more.

> *I think the American church has amnesia about a lot of this part of missions history.*

One organization called The Destiny Movement helps African Americans learn more about cross-cultural missions. In conjunction with InterVarsity Christian Fellowship, they put together a series of videos for churches specifically designed to call the African-American church back to missions. The videos point out that for various reasons from the mid-1900s on, the African-American church itself had amnesia about its heritage and interest in missions declined. Colonial governments refused to admit African-American missionaries from the West. United States missions agencies refused African-American candidates. Civil strife, especially in the South, forced the energy of the African-American church inward to survive. The many African Americans who moved north ended up focusing on the social concerns of the city and the ghetto.

Today, however, much has changed. Dr. Reuben Conner, who is the head of the National Black Evangelistic Association, says that the African-American church needs to renew its commitment to world evangelization. He tells the church that they have a special affinity to emerging nations because they understand their struggles. Dr. Conner is one of several powerful forces for missions in the African-American church. Great things are happening today.

The African-American mission situation is not the only one that is changing. There is great variety today in the "color" of missions. The team joining up for world evangelization is changing in many ways. One is the rise of Third-World mission agencies, and another is an increase in the number of missionaries who are not from the West. (To date, there are around 300,000 non-Western missionaries!) The church in the West was once considered the sending church, but now we are increasingly working hand-in-hand with many other nations towards world evangelization.

What advice would you give to the average white, suburban, middle class evangelical church that wants to be a part of the changing color of missions?

Adopt a sister church of another ethnic group.

My first and probably most achievable suggestion is for such a church to find a sister church close by—African-American, Korean, Spanish, Chinese, or other—and have members become involved in each others' lives and ministries. This happened in our church, and it was totally God's doing.

One time my friend Iain Crichton, a teacher at the Center for Urban Theological Studies in Philadelphia, asked me what my church was doing in the city. "Why are you only worrying about Turkey and China and Africa? What about Philadelphia?" he prodded. At that time I was missions chairman at a large suburban church north of Philadelphia. So I went home, looked through our budget, and saw we were doing nothing about Philadelphia. Later Iain told me about a church that was doing a good job of partnering with an inner-city church, and continued to challenge us in this area.

Interestingly enough, Philadelphia was one of the last cities that would allow African Americans to play on its major league baseball team. Finally, because Philadelphia had such a large African-American population, the Phillies had to sign some African Americans if they wanted any fans at the games. Before then, the only time the Philadelphia stands were packed was when Jackie Robinson came to town, and then everyone in Philly was cheering for his team, the Dodgers! That's Philadelphia!

> *There is great variety today in the "color" of missions.*

Now, back to my story. During the months when I was being prodded by Iain, God had our pastor "coincidentally" bump into the pastor of a small African-American inner-city church called Harambe Baptist Church. *Harambe* is the Swahili word for "pull together." Our pastor felt like we ought to help them. Then another man in our church told me we should get involved with this church. So I finally got the hint!

I thought we would be wasting our money and missing the boat if we just gave financially but never got personally involved. So I went down to see the pastor, Ted Johnson. The church sits right beside the state liquor store and across the street from the Voodoo Bar. This was a new setting for me, especially one for a church! The congregation had bought four or five garages and they were converting them into a church. I told Ted that we would like to offer them $2,500 and 2500 man-hours to start working together. We'd wanted them to also come up with 2500 man-hours. I said, "We want to learn from you, and share what we've learned with you. We don't want to be the big brother here; we want to work and learn together."

It really worked. Our pastors and choirs exchanged pulpits once in a while, and I'm here to tell you, when that choir came and Ted preached, our reserved white congregation rocked! Ted made it his goal to get some of these suburbanites to say "Amen." After one message, a woman came up to him and said, "I almost said it, pastor. You keep on; we'll get it."

Then our missions committee got a bright idea: Why not send Pastor Johnson to an ACMC conference? So Ted went to some conferences, and one day I got a paper from him in the mail entitled "Harambe Vision Paper Number One." It talked about the people they were sending on short-term missions that summer and outlined some of their missions goals.

And here's the icing on the cake: Ted sometimes teaches workshops with me on partnering with city churches. They have a small church but have sent their first missionary to Africa. Ted preaches missions and teaches missions. Not everything always went perfectly. There's been friction and misunderstandings. But we're a team and it's working.

Support international students interested in ministry.

Another significant way churches can play a part in the changing color of missions is to get involved with international students who are here studying for ministry. This is different than just getting involved with international students in general. Many churches are near seminaries and Christian universities where leaders from the church in Third-World countries have come to get advanced degrees. Here's an opportunity to take three or four years to get to know a Third-World church leader and his or her family, and then have a strong foundation for providing continuing support.

Even if your church is not near one of these schools, write

and ask them to recommend an international student for your missions conference. Build relationships. At the rate people fly around the world these days, keeping in touch with these men and women is not the concern it once was. Have a business executive in your church who is flying to Rome, stop in and see your international missionary in Crete. The world is smaller these days.

Let me tell you about one international student we had the privilege of supporting. We met Sam Ngewa while he was in Philadelphia studying for his Ph.D. at Westminster Theological Seminary. Now he is teaching theology at Nairobi Evangelical Graduate School of Theology in Kenya. I'll always remember Sam as "the African who bought a church for an American congregation." It's one of my favorite stories.

Sam and his wife, Elizabeth, were attending a small but very missions-minded church here in the States. It was a new fellowship, and the 150 or so people were meeting in a rented warehouse in a small town. The warehouse custodian didn't like them meeting there and would show up late to unlock the building and do whatever he could to make life miserable for the people. The church was growing and was giving more than 70 percent of its money to missions. (Now that church supports Sam and Elizabeth in Kenya.) Things were going from bad to worse at the warehouse, so they decided to pray and seek God on the matter. They absolutely did not want to get involved in a building program because they felt committed to putting most of their money into missions.

One weekend, one of the elders heard about a church nearby that was struggling. Only about twenty people were left in its membership. So Sam's church decided to ask if they could rent the church's facilities on Sunday afternoons. They thought the rent might help that church.

When the fellowship approached the people of this church, the response was amazing. They said, "Last night we had a meeting and decided to close the church. We can no longer operate it. We'll give you the building, since it will be used as a church. But in order to make it legal, we'll have to sell it to you for one dollar." Well, Sam had the dollar in his pocket, and he bought the building right then and there.

It is such a joy to see what happens when a church commits itself to God and to world evangelization. God blesses the giving and going church.

Tell us about the other side of the story—Third World missions and mission agencies. That's part of the changing color of missions, too, isn't it?

This is the real World Series. It's looking ahead to the future. It's where missions is headed. Let's take a look at some questions that come up in relation to this growing area of missions outreach in other parts of the world and discuss the part to be played by the North American church.

Question 1: What is nationalizing?

Everyone wants to know how nationalizing a work begun by missionaries works. It's one of those buzz words that comes up when you're with missions types. Should we just call the American missionary force home, lock, stock, and barrel? Some missiologists would like us to believe that's the best thing that could happen to Third-World churches. Some talk about the fact that a significant number of missionaries are ineffective or have overstayed their usefulness. There is some truth in that statement. Sometimes missionaries say, "Maybe if we all just came home, the international church would grow faster and mature more quickly."

On the other hand, I was recently in Kenya talking with some of the faculty at Scott Theological College in Machakos.

Scott is a university level, degree-granting Bible College. The principal is Dr. Julius Muthergi, who received his doctorate from Trinity International University, and the leadership and the entire board is Kenyan. The faculty is 50 percent Kenyan and 50 percent missionary. I asked the expatriate professors if the college was looking forward to the day when it would be totally nationalized. They said no. They need a global perspective, new ideas from the West, and the fresh blood internationals bring. They want crosspollination with the thinking that goes on all over the world.

> *Third-World missions is becoming the real World Series. It's looking ahead to the future. It's where missions is headed.*

We also have to look at the importance to the West of sending people to serve. If we stop sending people to support nationals, we will lose touch with what is happening there, and the interest in missions will dry up. We have to give our people, not just our money. I'm convinced that's biblical. The Bible doesn't say "Send money"; it says "Go."

Question 2: What is a "missionary" anymore?

Many people in the West have trouble grasping the idea that we are no longer doing grassroots pioneer missions in many parts of the world. Many ministries are now run by national leaders and a large number of missionaries are involved in training and support ministries. Perhaps we want to picture our missionary outside a grass hut or under a banana tree telling people about Jesus (and that is still happening). But the reality is that many missionaries are lecturing at a university, leading a lunchtime Bible study for businesspeople in a high-rise office, or repairing a plane or a computer system. If a missionary can do a job that enables a national believer to be more effective, then that's what he or she should do.

Fifty percent of the world's population now lives in cities and most city dwellers live in high-rise housing. With the rate of urbanization in the world, most of our missionaries in the next generation will be living in apartments in large cities. That may be hard for many of us to visualize. The exciting challenge for the church in coming years is that whatever a person's career or calling, there's a place to serve in missions.

Question 3: With far-flung international partnerships, what about accountability?

North Americans like to see bottom-line reports and know what bang they will get for their buck. There is one Third-World mission agency that I believe provides a great model of partnership that continues to work. Lawrence Bomett, a Kenyan student, got a master's degree at Trinity International University in Illinois. In one class, Paul Hiebert, chairman of the missions department, gave an assignment to develop a proposal for a mission agency. They were to write its purpose statement, goals, strategies, and methods for implementing ministry. Lawrence designed an organization called Africans Reaching Africa (ARA). When Dr. Hiebert saw the proposal, he urged Lawrence to make this happen and offered to be on his board of directors.

Lawrence went through with it and the agency has been growing now for a few years. It has a U.S. board of directors which includes investment counselors, attorneys, pastors, professors, and businesspeople. It also has a committee in England and an advisory board in Africa made up of attorneys, businessmen, missionaries, and pastors. ARA is registered and incorporated in the United States and in Kenya as a nonprofit organization.

The support from the West for ARA is matched dollar-for-dollar by African churches. The long-term goal of this approach is to help existing African mission agencies succeed when finances are a struggle. More than that, the organization is committed to teaching African churches how to give, and they have recently hired a man who does something like I do, visiting churches to motivate them in missions. The incentive is that their giving will be matched by the church worldwide. It must be working—in 1995, ARA doubled the number of African missionaries they supported, from twenty to forty. I believe some of this is because of the high level of openness and accountability in the organization.

Question 4: What does internationalization of missions mean?

American mission agencies are becoming the national offices that are part of larger international and worldwide agencies, with headquarters just about anywhere. The "Protestant Vatican" may no longer be in Wheaton, Illinois, or Colorado Springs, Colorado. Maybe many Christian agencies will soon have their headquarters in Nairobi, Kenya, or Seoul, Korea. We need to think now about what structures are needed for supporting international leadership.

> *The "Protestant Vatican" may no longer be in Wheaton or Colorado Springs. Many Christian agencies may soon have their headquarters in Nairobi or Seoul.*

This is a challenge for the church today. Where will the center for world missions outreach be? How will American local churches get strategically involved? American businesses are facing these same challenges as corporations go global and headquarters get moved all over the world. It's an exciting change to think about.

Question 5: What does tentmaking mean in missions today?

Tentmaking is not a new idea—after all the apostle Paul did it. As times change, though, so does the form of our self-supporting missions work. Young people are going to China to teach English as a second language in the universities. Perhaps this does not fit old stereotypes of a missionary, but it is one exciting way to look at serving.

Let me tell you one story about a tentmaker/English teacher. One day a woman named Sue phoned me from State College, Pennsylvania. She had been in a "Perspectives on the World Christian Movement" class, a course sponsored by the U.S. Center for World Mission and which I participated in. Sue said, "Tom you don't know me, but I was in that Perspectives class. I'm going to China, and I need $500."

"Sister, you're out of your mind," I said. "You don't go to my church and I don't even know you. I'll do this for you, though—you come and talk to me, and I will listen to you. Just remember, we do not give money out like that."

She did come see me and impressed me with all she knew about China as just a college senior at the time. I asked her to come to our church and talk about China for three minutes. She came, and at the end of the three minutes, my pastor asked her to keep talking. We could feel the Spirit of God working though that young woman and we ended up supporting her. Sue mentored a number of other people in our church who considered China, and today our church has at least ten people in China as tentmaker missionaries. They work in Holiday Inns, in schools, and in colleges. What incredible involvement we have there for a small sum of support!

The greatest part of this story, however, is that in the third year that Sue Jacobson was teaching in Beijing University, she was asked to teach American culture besides English. She asked the department head if she could teach something from the Bible because that was a part of American culture. He agreed. So Sue did a course on the Gospel of John. Her final question on the exam was, "Will you accept Jesus Christ as your personal Savior?" Nine people in that class accepted Christ, and very soon one of those men began leading a house church. This also led to one of her students coming to the States to study. I'll never forget Little John standing in front of our church telling us how he accepted Jesus Christ as a result of that exam.

All of these advances in international missions and collaborative efforts around the world are some of the reasons why I think I'm in the best job there is. We need to let God direct our churches to move into areas of world evangelization that we never dreamed possible. The creative possibilities are limitless, as long as we remember that all of our plans and schemes are nothing without the work of the Holy Spirit. It's great to be working to fulfill what's at the heart of God's intention for the world—that people from every tribe and nation will fall down and worship Jesus, his Son.

FAN FARE

Home Run News

One of my best memories is playing ball in high school. I made the varsity team as a freshman and played left field. We won the county championship that year. I played left field again in my sophomore year. In my most memorable accomplishment of all four years, I smashed a home run over the fence in deep right field.

Actually, I never saw the ball clear the fence, because I was running for all I was worth. As I approached third base, I could see my coach, Amos Herr, jumping up and down, yelling, and waving his hat. Not until I crossed the plate did I realize that I could have waltzed around the bases, because the ball was long gone over the fence.

What made this home run extra delicious was the fact that I connected off Ray Kreider, an all-star fastball pitcher who scared the socks off of us. That was the first and only home run of my high school career. We lost that game, but what a thrill.

I learned later my home run was a prodigious "shot heard around the world." The local newspaper printed an article about my smash hit, along with my picture, and the paper was sent abroad to the servicemen serving in World War II at that time. I had made world news.

—*James Reapsome, editor-at-large for* Evangelical Missions Quarterly *and* World Pulse Newsletter

8
Staying with the Fundamentals

Biblical Truths to Keep You Motivated

"Missions is on every page of the Bible. It starts in Genesis and is wrapped up in Revelation, when the whole world will be worshiping Jesus."

Many people say Earl Weaver of the Baltimore Orioles was the best manager in baseball. I think they are right. He managed for twenty-seven years and in twenty-one of those years his club finished first or second. He didn't always have the greatest players either; he just knew how to manage them.

Weaver was a genius about the game. To him, there was a right way to do things. He believed in the fundamentals and stuck with them. He called the fundamentals the "inner game." Similarly, that's how I look at the biblical truths of the gospel—they are the "inner game" that keep me motivated in missions.

What are some of the fundamentals of your missions game?

I don't want to sound like I have it all together by any means. Weaver used to say, "It's what you learn after you know it all that counts." I'm still learning every day what the inner game is, and I'm trying to understand more deeply the essential truths on which our lives and vision must be built. I try to read everything and anything I can about missions. A list of many of the books I recommend is in the back of this book. But it's the Bible that keeps me focused.

> *I believe the Bible is a missionary book all the way through.*

I get so discouraged when I hear people talk as if there is only one missionary passage in Scripture: Matthew 28:19-20, the great commission. I believe the Bible is a missionary book all the way through, from Genesis to Revelation. I want to mention here four fundamental truths that keep me motivated. They are the foundation on which everything I do is built.

Fundamental #1: God is a missionary God.

God has recorded throughout Scripture his heart for the nations. Someone challenged me once to do a study of the word "nations" in the Bible. Starting with Genesis 12, where God told Abraham he would be a blessing to the nations, I saw that God's plan from square one was to call fallen people back to himself. Later he showed Abraham all the stars in the night sky and said his children would be like that. Well, *we* are those children and we are on God's heart.

What does that mean for us today as children of Abraham? In order to be a blessing, we need God's heart for the nations.

Some people call this theme the ribbon of redemption; but whatever you call it, it means that God is bringing people back to himself through his Word, his Son, and in our generation, the church.

Another important missionary verse that demonstrates God's heart is 1 Timothy 2:4. It says that God desires that all people come to salvation. That sounds like a missionary call to me. We have something in umpiring that says, "Keep the strike zone consistent." Similarly, I think if we keep within this first fundamental zone, that God is a missionary God, it keeps us from getting distracted by other things that aren't priorities. Sometimes I go into churches and they are so busy—programs are going on, committees are meeting, there is activity everywhere. My question is, how much of this activity is going on outside the crucial strike zone?

John Piper, the pastor of Bethlehem Baptist Church in Minneapolis, has written an outstanding book on missions called, *Let the Nations Be Glad: The Supremacy of God in Missions*. He reminds us that if we're not excited about God, and if we don't rejoice in who God is, then how can we have enough joy to carry out the missionary task? Piper calls for a God-centered motivation for doing world evangelization.

This reminds me of a comment a young woman in our church made in a missions prayer meeting, "I hope we never get so excited about missions that we overlook Jesus." Missions cannot be an end in itself or we will fail big time. The Lord God has to be our ultimate motivation for missions.

Fundamental #2: Jesus is God's missionary Son.

What greater example could there be for sending our best people than God's willingness to send his Son to save the world? Jesus provided the only means for salvation. If there was another way, why should we bother sending missionaries to share the news? But there is no other way.

We all love those services where parents dedicate their children to the Lord. It's exciting to see the new little person prayed for, even if he is crying and drooling in front of the church. In many churches, the pastors ask the congregation to stand and say that they will consider it their responsibility to rear this child in the likeness of Christ.

But where are these parents and church people when it's time to say that we'll give our children for the sake of the gospel to world missions, or that we will disciple our children to consider becoming missionaries? What might happen if some Christian parents told their children, "When you were a baby we gave you to the Lord. Unless God leads you otherwise, we are praying that you will consider missions." Now there's something to think about. We need to give our sons and daughters the way God the Father gave his.

> **We need to give our sons and daughters the way God the Father gave his.**

Fundamental #3: The Bible is a missionary book.

If you approach the Bible with your heart set on finding missions in it, you will be absolutely amazed. Missions is on every page. It starts in Genesis and is wrapped up in those climactic verses in Revelation, when the whole world will be worshiping Jesus.

There's God's first promise to Abraham in Genesis 12 that he would be a blessing to the nations, but keep reading. About halfway through the Bible, you'll find another promise in Habbakuk 2:14 that says, "The earth will be filled with the knowledge of the glory of the LORD, as the waters cover the sea." Skip on over to the end with that thrilling chorus of praise to the Lamb in Revelation 5:9: "You are worthy to take the scroll and to open its seals, because you were slain, and with your blood you purchased men for God from every tribe and language and people and nation." There are myriad references to God's great redemptive plan. Almost every book in the Bible has many missions-related references. I challenge you to look at the Bible with a missions vision and you will be surprised.

Fundamental #4: The church has a missionary mandate.

I will spend more time on this fundamental because my work and personal call is to motivate the church for world evangelization. Kenneth Strachan, former director of the Latin American Mission, observed:

> Every Christian, regardless of his position, is faced with a mission that does not permit him to hide inside sheltering walls, but thrusts him out into the world; into its outermost parts. Christ committed to his church the task of proclaiming the Gospel to every creature among all nations, to the uttermost part of the earth and to the end of the age. (From *Strachan on Costa Rica* by Dayton Roberts)

Obedience to the command in Matthew 28:19-20 must have a top priority. It is not a suggestion—it's a command. Since the church at Antioch sent Paul and Barnabas out as recorded in Acts 13, every local church has had the responsibility for being the primary sending base for missions outreach around the world. The gospel is spread to every continent and nation through men and women who have been called of God and sent by local bodies of believers to take the message of Christ to people in other cultures.

What really bothers me is that only a small minority of local churches have a vision of what God wants to do through them. John Bennett of ACMC says that there are 300,000 churches in America and yet only 10 percent have a missions program. To be perfectly frank, I think there may be far fewer than 10 percent of churches with missions programs. Some churches say they have missions programs because they send a token 5 percent of their budget to some denominational or church agency, and then wash their hands of further responsibility. Sorry, but that's not missions.

I would like to challenge churches that have effective, growing missions programs to help other churches in their neighborhood. Missions isn't competition. Churches need to cooperate with one another to get the job done. Of course, it's easy to imagine a few problems here. What if churches don't have the same vision, or what if they differ in various beliefs? Yet, for the sake of world evangelization, we need to build bridges and surmount these. When you have a mandate from God, you work out the problems. I have some personal experience in this area.

> *Missions isn't competition. Churches need to cooperate with one another to get the job done.*

My father was a pastor in a very conservative church and was still preaching at age ninety-two. So I was reared in an independent church setting. When I was called to work with ACMC, they sent me to address a United Church of Christ. Because I had been raised with the idea that any church that wasn't doing things the way we did was going to end up in hell, I went to that church with all kinds of misconceptions. But when I walked in the door, things changed. The missions committee had already started the meeting and they were praying. As I listened, I realized they were praying no differently than the people prayed back at my father's church. They were praying to the same Lord. They were agonizing over lost souls. Seeing the essentials of faith helps us work together.

But there are some obstacles churches face on the way to fulfilling their missionary mandate together.

1. We get hung up on less important theological issues. Protestant churches tend not to cooperate with Catholics. Evangelicals move in different directions than liberals. Many conservatives are not comfortable with charismatics, and fundamentalists prefer to work separately. In the last year I have consulted with Presbyterian, Baptist, charismatic, Methodist churches, and more. I once spoke at a large Episcopalian church outside of Washington, D.C., and my wife, who is from an even more conservative background than I am, experienced one of the most meaningful Communion services she had ever been in. Let's not get hung up on aspects of doctrine that are not essentials of the faith.

2. Differences between churches are often cultural, not necessarily doctrinal. I visit churches where they believe they haven't had a church service if they don't sing three hymns and have somebody sing a solo before the message. Choosing to worship with incense, bells, liturgy, or praise music is often a cultural choice. Having the preacher wear a robe and a collar is cultural. Forbidding the use of musical instruments on the basis of the New Testament church, or replacing an organ with guitars is a cultural choice.

Every church meets a need in a cultural context, whether it be the culture imagined in the New Testament, the culture of the church founders, or the culture of the modern boomer or buster. For the sake of world evangelization, I believe we have to get over our problems with some of this.

3. Churches are too inward-focused. They are not willing to help other churches because they are turned in toward themselves. They worship the culture of their church instead of worshiping the Christ of the church. Perhaps part of the problem is a fear that there are only so many people and so many funds to draw from to support our individual ministries. But when you look through history at times when God poured out his Spirit in an area or country, people were not worrying about where a fellowworker was from or what agency he was with; the most important thing was getting the gospel out.

> **Many churches worship the culture of their church instead of worshiping the Christ of the church.**

The recent baseball strike should help us stop and think. If players and owners would have worked together, we would not have lost a whole year of baseball. Sometimes I wonder if we have lost a whole year in the spread of the gospel because local churches can't work together. More scary than that—would we even know it if we did lose a year in world evangelization? The biblical truth is that the more we give away, the more we will be blessed. I wish churches could see that truth.

Paul McKaughan, president of EFMA, has said a disturbing thing:

> Without massive re-ordering of the U.S. missionary enterprise and a dynamic movement of the Spirit of God renewing his church, the structures and industry which we represent will, in the not too distant future, appear analogous to an abandoned ship buried in the tides of a sandy seashore with only the weather-beaten ribs as visible testimony to a far better and more useful day.

We have to take warnings like that to heart. But on the other hand, we have to remember that we are not responsible for the whole enterprise, only for doing what God calls us to do.

4. Getting started is the hardest part. I once conducted a workshop on the ten components of a successful missions program in an influential church in the Midwest. They had all the ideas down, but I got the distinct feeling it was never going to happen. They would talk a lot, but never get going. Since we know our common goal is the great commission—reaching the world for Jesus Christ—perhaps what we need to do is take just one step in that direction and see what happens.

A few years ago I spoke at a United Church of Christ in New England. After I shared about organizing for missions in your local church, a woman came up and asked me to pray for her. I asked why. She said, "I'm in a church where the missions budget last year was $100." Then she said, "We didn't spend all of it."

She said she would go back to her church and try to follow some of my suggestions and what she had learned at the seminar. Six months later I got a phone call from her. They had their first missions conference planned and she wanted me to come speak. When I agreed to come and asked how things were going, she said the missions budget was up to $3,000. They had started a missions committee and they had found another couple of churches in the area to work with.

When I came for the conference, I found that they had invited all the churches within a thirty-mile radius to come, and fifteen of those churches showed up. There were Baptists sitting beside Presbyterians and Methodists and all the rest of them. This church is trying to get that whole community concerned about missions. The last time I talked to her, their missions budget was over $30,000! This was a church in rural New Hampshire just getting started in missions. They didn't complain about being small or about not having enough money; they just went to work.

Try it. Next time your church rents a missionary film, or pays to have a key speaker, invite everyone in the neighborhood. Invite women's and men's groups from another church to your missions conference. Invite people from another church to your missions committee meeting as you strategize. Phone four or five churches in your neighborhood, find out who the missions person is in that church, and ask how you can help him or her. Open up the discussion by asking, "How's your missions program? What are you doing that works? This is what we are doing," and build some kind of relationship with them. Then be willing to stand alongside and help them. If you start doing that just because you want to see more churches involved in missions, you will see results, I guarantee it. But get started.

If there was one last thing you could say about the church's mandate to be a missionary church, what would it be?

Missions needs to be integrated into the decision and commitment of every new believer. When we lead people to Christ we need to tell them right off that their commitment is to Christ as King of their lives. It is also a commitment to his people, to his Word, and to the church. We must be absolutely clear that they have marching orders to obey the great commission. We don't say that enough. The marching orders are for every Christian.

> *Our marching orders to obey the great commission are for every Christian. We don't say that enough.*

You see, we often say to people, "Believe these four things and then you are saved." Then about a month later we say, "Oh, and by the way, you need to go to church about five times a week; you need to give 10 percent of your income to the church; and you may end up in China." It's like the fast-talking insurance man who comes to my house and makes me sign stuff and then tells me what's in the fine print. That's no way to lead people to Christ. We need to be up front and tell them what it really means to be a disciple of Christ. They have to consider world evangelization as one part of their commitment to Christ.

It costs something to become a Christian—our whole lives. I wonder what it would be like if every new believer understood from day one that missions is not just another program in the life of the church; missions *is* the church. That's the fundamental truth.

FAN FARE

Religion as Baseball

Calvinists believe the game is fixed.

Lutherans believe they can't win, but trust the Score-keeper.

Quakers won't swing the bat.

Unitarians can catch anything, but can't find the right ballpark.

The Amish walk a lot.

Pagans sacrifice.

Jehovah's Witnesses are thrown out often.

Televangelists get caught stealing.

Episcopalians pass the plate.

Evangelicals make effective pitches.

Fundamentalists balk.

Mormons are in left field.

Independents are in right field.

Dunkers are down by three.

Adventists have a seventh-inning stretch.

Atheists refuse to have an Umpire.

Baptists want to play hardball.

Premillennialists expect the game to be called soon on account of darkness.

Postmillennialists keep looking for the game to finally be perfected.

Amillennialists just keep on playing and playing and playing.

Methodists get traded every two years.

Preterists already know the final score.

The pope never commits an error.

—*author unknown*

9
The Hall of Fame

Churches with Top-Notch Missions Programs

"Missions is not just one of the church's many programs; it is the mandate of the church."

When a bunch of baseball fans get together, discussion usually gets around to "What are the greatest teams of all time?" Whenever that argument gets going, you hear names like the 1927 Yankees, the 1912 Red Sox, the 1975 Cincinnati Reds (that's *the Red Machine*), and the 1972 Oakland As. There have to be criteria for judging who is the greatest, and the standard measure is winning over a hundred games. There are some good ways to measure where churches are in missions too.

What would you consider the criteria for judging the top missions-minded churches in America today?

I've often been asked that kind of question because I'm in and out of churches every week. My purpose is always the same—to motivate churches in missions. So I have my opinions, I'll admit that, and my umpiring experience can help me deal with any resulting controversy! But before I even get into that, I can honestly say that my top church of all time was the New Testament church at Antioch.

There are many things I like about the church in Antioch. This was a church that was born because of evangelism. They were a giving church and had an outward focus. They were missions-minded, and throughout the book of Acts they show up as the church that sent out its own people. They also chose their best people to go.

> *The church in Antioch was missions-minded and sent their best people out. If every church had those two criteria, we'd get the job done.*

It seems that churches are often reluctant to give the Lord their best people. We talk about first fruits in our offering of money, but what about the best of our sons and daughters when it comes to those we give to the Lord for his mission of world evangelization? If every church had those two criteria—to be known as a missions church and to send the best—we'd get the job done! The church in Antioch was also the first church to have a missions conference (see Acts 14:27-28). It is a great example.

From my personal experience, let me give you my criteria for a top-notch missions program. Then I'll list the churches I feel are the best ones meeting those criteria.

1. The church must have an outward focus and strategy. Some churches have great difficulty in getting the congregation to vote for spending money on projects or programs that don't benefit them directly. In a culture that says, "He who dies with the most toys wins," it can be a struggle.

2. *At least 30 percent of the church's budget must go to missions.* This comes from a solid commitment to missions and provides a true example of giving to church members. Many churces do far better, with up to 75 percent of budget going to cross-cultural ministry.

3. *The church must have an ongoing training program for missionary candidates.* This is not a quick, two-week thing in the spring. This preparation and training in ministry should be part of a continuous year-round program. (See chapter 3 for my discussion on this.)

4. *Missions education must be integrated through all the programs of the church.* Sunday school, Vacation Bible School, youth group, choir, Pioneer Clubs, and Awana—whatever is going on in your church must be flavored with missions. The people need to be constantly aware that missions is not just one of the church's many programs; it is the mandate of the church.

5. *The church must be sending its own people.* I was at a big missions conference of an active church and asked the pastor how many of the missionaries were from their church. The answer was not one. That is not a healthy sign.

6. *The church must be concerned about and pray for the lost.* You might think this is hard to determine, but when I'm in different churches Sunday after Sunday, I soon pick up on where the heart of the people is. When you hear kids in first grade, with no prompting, pray for their unsaved schoolmates and pray for missionaries who are in unreached areas, you know something good is going on.

7. *The church must have a pastor who leads them in vision and outreach.* It's just one of the facts of church life—as the pastor goes, so goes the church. The pulpit is the control center of the church, and if the pastor is missions-minded, the people will catch the vision. There's no way around that fact.

8. *The church must be interested in helping other churches in missions.* By this I mean, the church can partnership with

inner-city churches or neighborhood churches. This could mean banding with the church up the street to bring in a speaker or sharing a missions training program with a church that doesn't have the resources or personnel.

9. *The church must have a strong evangelism program in its community.* If people are concerned about their friends and neighbors here, they will be interested in reaching out cross-culturally around the world too. I always say, "The light that shines the farthest shines the brightest close to home."

> ***The light that shines the farthest shines the brightest close to home.***

Rick Warren says in his book, *The Purpose-Driven Church,* that "a great commitment to the Great Commandment and the Great Commission will grow a great church." I hope my few insights presented here will strengthen your missions commitment. There's no greater work to be done than spreading the good news of Christ. Is your church getting into the game?

What are your top missions-minded churches in the United States right now?

As soon as I give you my top list, you'll think of a church that should have been included. It's the same with the All Star game in the middle of the baseball season. Does everyone agree on the players picked for that game? Never! So this is my list, in alphabetical order, and I'll take responsibility for it.

Bethlehem Baptist Church in Minneapolis, Minnesota

This church has a great training program for future missionaries; they are a model of a church that prays for missions. They have a goal to send out 200 missionaries by the year 2000, and they are moving quickly toward that goal. They have an excellent, well-formed missions policy.

Black Rock Congregational Church in Fairfield, Connecticut

They have one of the best missions conferences I know of. Members there might miss the Christmas pageant and the Easter cantata, but not the missions conference. People come from far and wide to attend it. They have faith-promise giving of over half a million dollars, and this is from an 800-member church. They have adopted an unreached people group and have a powerful prayer emphasis for missions in the church. Every program and ministry in the church has a missions focus integrated into it.

Briarwood Presbyterian Church in Birmingham, Alabama

This church built a multimillion dollar building and increased missions giving at the same time. They have an outstanding *two-week* missions conference. (Some churches do well to have a two-day conference.) They also have a strong missions emphasis from the pulpit. Forty-five percent of their million-dollar budget is for missions, and they are helping neighborhood churches get turned on to missions.

Calvary Church in Lancaster, Pennsylvania

This church has a million-dollar missions budget and a great prayer emphasis. They support many of their missionaries at 75 percent. Over 50 percent of their budget goes toward missions. They have also adopted a people group in Macedonia.

Candia Congregational Church in Candia, New Hampshire

Even though this is a small, rural church, the congregation does things a lot of large churches won't even attempt. They are a very missions-motivated church. With about 150 members, they have everyone involved. They have adopted a people group, and they do lots of short-term missions work. The pastor is sold out for missions. This church is also a tremendous example of involving the neighborhood churches and sharing everything they learn. They give far more than they can afford.

The Christian Fellowship Church in Evansville, Indiana

This church is the model of a church that supports members in missions work. The average support per couple is $30,000. They are a very caring church, and they are very creative in mobilizing other churches around them to become missions-minded. The pastor is an effective role model.

Church of the Savior in Wayne, Pennsylvania

This congregation is doing a progressive job in missions. They have adopted a people group in Indonesia. They hold a dynamic missions conference and run a parallel children's missions conference that the kids love. They have a strong missions budget.

Church on Brady in Los Angeles, California

This Southern Baptist church has more missionaries on the mission field than any other Southern Baptist church in America, yet it is not one of their largest churches. It is an urban church enthusiastic about church planting at home and overseas. Their Christian education/missions program for children is well-integrated, and they are doing an effective job of turning baby boomers and busters on to missions.

College Church in Wheaton, Illinois

A competent missions team strategically invests more than one million dollars annually in missions (approaching 50 percent of their total budget). It has a long history of missions commitment.

The Elmbrook Church in Waukesha, Wisconsin

This church has a number of partnerships with other churches. They have adopted a people group. They have an excellent faith-promise giving program which has resulted in a large, growing missions budget nearing one and a half million dollars. They also have a solid training program and missions conference. They support more than 130 missionaries.

Emmanuel Faith Community Church in Escondido, California

This church has strong missions leadership. They have an active short-term missions program and training programs. They host the Perspectives on the World Christian Movement course to teach their people and other churches in the area the basics in missions awareness. They are committed to excellence and hold their missionaries accountable.

The Evangelical Free Church of Hershey, Pennsylvania

Missions is what this church is all about. They care for their missionaries and hold them accountable. Forty percent of their budget goes to missions. They have a model missions policy and a very active missions subcommittee setup. When this church was going into a major building project, the pastor had to run a parallel missions project of the same amount. He told me, "I have to do it this way or the people won't give to the building." That's healthy stuff.

Evergreen Southern Baptist Church in Rosemead, California

This church has forty-six missions teams involved in local and international missions. They are a wonderful example of a congregation in which every member is involved in world evangelization.

Family Bible Church in Willow Grove, Pennsylvania

This is a smaller church, but its whole focus and purpose is to support world missions. The families are missions-minded. They have unique missions conferences and give a large percentage of their budget to missions. They support Third-World missionaries.

Grace Chapel in Lexington, Massachusetts

This church is committed to educating their own people and the churches in their region about missions strategies and goals. Their missions pastor is innovative and keeps the people growing and informed as world Christians. They have a sister church in the CIS (the old USSR), and send out twenty short-term mission teams.

Hinson Memorial Baptist in Portland, Oregon

This church has an excellent program for training missionary candidates. They are committed to developing world Christians in their local church. They have one of the leading faith-promise programs in the United States.

Northside Community Church in Atlanta, Georgia

More than 150 of their people have been to Bosnia. In fact,

they have a team working there at all times. They have planted two missions-motivated daughter churches in Atlanta. They have become their own sending agency and much more. This church is an exciting place to be.

Overlake Christian Church in Kirkland, Washington

Overlake has a million dollar budget, and the congregation also takes on a lot of large missions projects. Using many of their own businesspeople, they are very successful in finding innovative ways to help Third-World people establish and run businesses. They send out a lot of effective short-term teams.

Pascack Bible Church in Hillsdale, New Jersey

This church has a strong commitment to missions on the pastoral staff. They have adopted a people group, and they have a well-developed missions strategy and excellent missions conferences. A high percentage of their total budget goes to missions.

Spanish River Presbyterian Church in Boca Raton, Florida

This is a model church for supporting Third-World church planters. They also plant a new church in the United States every year. Annually at their missions conference they bring in all the church planters they support from around the world and share ideas and encourage one another. Many of these are Third-World pastors and church planters so the ideas and sharing are especially rich. This also helps them ensure accountability when dealing with the support of far-flung personnel.

Wooddale Church in Eden Prairie, Minnesota

This church always has an exciting missions conference.

They send a lot of their people overseas on short-term projects to increase the vision of the church body. They have adopted a people group and give a high percentage of their budget to missions. The pastor is sold out to missions. They have developed an excellent missions strategy.

Bibliography

Tom's Required Reading List

I hope these suggestions will encourage more reading in missions. Missions is a life-long process. Never, never, never stop reading!

I. Suggested Reading

Bonk, Jonathan. *Missions and Money*. Deals with affluence as a missionary problem for the westerner.

Borthwick, Paul. *A Mind for Missions*. A must read for anyone interested in missions. Many missions committees require this for new committee members.

_____. *Six Dangerous Questions*. Deals with how to transform your world view.

Bryant, David. *In the Gap*. Comes with a study guide. Asks a lot of hard questions. Great for new missions committee members.

Covey, Stephen. *The Seven Habits of Highly Effective People*. I'm still convinced that if we don't learn how to manage ourselves and those we lead, the missionary cause will be greatly hindered. This book helps.

Elmer, Duane. *Cross-Cultural Conflict*. Excellent insight on how to handle cultural challenges and problems.

Hale, Tom. *Don't Let the Goats Eat the Loquat Trees*. Great story of missionary life in Nepal.

Johnstone, Patrick. *Operation World*. Must sit next to the Bible in every Christian's home. A very informative day-to-day prayer guide for world missions.

McQuilkin, Robertson. *The Great Omission*. This book deals with the question of why many Christians are not involved in missions.

Murray, Andrew. *Key to the Missionary Problem*. A classic. An "oldy but goody" that must be read.

Piper, John. *Let the Nations Be Glad: The Supremacy of God in Missions*. Absolute must for pastors. Great biblical perspective on why we do missions. Goes beyond the Great Commission.

Pirolo, Neal. *Serving as Senders*. Excellent book for the home team. Full of help for the "senders" of missionaries.

Plueddemann, Jim and Carol. *Witnesses to All the World*. Nine-session inductive Bible studyguide exploring God's heart for missions woven throughout the Scriptures.

Raymo, James. *Marching to a Different Drummer*. Rediscovering missions in an age of affluence and self-interest. Deals with problems 1990s Christians face when they want to get involved in missions.

Richardson, Don. *Peace Child; Eternity in Their Hearts; Lords of the Earth*. These three books are all excellent stories that communicate important concepts for missions vision and strategy.

Saal, William. *Reaching Muslims for Christ*. Written for the average Christian. Help for reaching out to Muslims at home and overseas.

Stearns, Bill and Amy. *Catch the Vision 2000*. Great book for new believers. Explains how to reach the unreached and why we should be involved.

Tucker, Ruth. *From Jerusalem to Irian Jaya*. One of the best missions history books. Enjoyable reading. (Even with the omissions I mentioned in chapter seven!)

Ward, Ted. *Living Overseas*. Even if you're not going overseas, it is a great way to help you understand and pray for those who are. Fun and informational.

Winter, Ralph, and Hawthorne, Stephen. *Perspectives on the World Christian Movement*. This book covers missions from A to Z. No self-respecting missions person should be without it.

II. Special Recommendations

If I could put one book on missions into every pastor's hand it would be *Let the Nations Be Glad* by John Piper. I believe it would transform the missionary enterprise in America.

If I could give two books to every missions chairperson I meet, they would be *The Top Ten Mistakes Leaders Make* by Hans Finzel, and *Cultivating a Missions Active Church* produced by ACMC.

If I could give three books to every missionary going overseas, they would be *Overcoming Missionary Stress* by Marjory Foyle, *Sojourners* by Ruth and Sam Rowen, and *Cross-Cultural Conflict* by Duane Elmer.

III. The ACMC list of recommended books for people interested in world evangelization

Fascinating missionary reading for the family:
Partee, Charles. *Adventure in Africa.*
Olson, Bruce. *Bruchko.*
Stafford, Tim. *The Friendship Gap.*
Tucker, Ruth. *From Jerusalem to Irian Jaya.*
Anderson, Neil. *In Search of the Source.*
Hale, Thomas. *Living Stones of the Himalayas.*
St. Kilda, Martin. *Near the Far Bamboo.*
Hale, Thomas. *On the Far Side of Liglig Mountain.*
Richardson, Don. *Peace Child.*

On communicating to contemporary Christians:
Peterson, Jim. *Church without Walls.*
Newbigin, Lesslie. *Foolishness to the Greeks.*
Newbigin, Lesslie. *The Gospel in a Pluralist Society.*
Hunter, George. *How to Reach Secular People.*
Strobel, Lee. *Inside the Mind of Unchurched Harry and Mary.*
Ford, Kevin. *Jesus for a New Generation.*

On the impact of culture on the church:
Carter, Stephen. *Culture of Disbelief.*
Hunter, James D. *Culture Wars.*
Zacharias, Ravi. *Deliver Us from Evil.*
Guinness, Os. *Dining with the Devil.*
Wells, David. *God in the Wasteland.*
Bonk, Jonathan. *Missions and Money.*

On contextualizing the church for the culture:
Anderson, Leith. *A Church for the Twenty-First Century.*
Hunter, George. *Church for the Unchurched.*

George, Carl. *The Coming Church Revolution.*
Anderson, Lynn. *Navigating Change.*
Schaller, Lyle. *The New Reformation.*
Malphurs, Aubrey. *Pouring New Wine into Old Wineskins.*
Warren, Rick. *The Purpose-Driven Church.*
Schaller, Lyle. *Strategies for Change.*
McIntosh, Gary. *Three Generations.*

On leadership management for progress in missions:
Covey, Stephen. *Built to Last.*
Covey, Stephen. *First Things First.*
Bennis, Warren. *Leaders.*
DePree, Max. *Leadership Jazz.*
Peters, Tom. *Liberation Management.*
Drucker, Peter F. *Managing in a Time of Great Change.*
Covey, Stephen. *Principle-Centered Leadership.*
Finzel, Hans. *Top Ten Mistakes Leaders Make.*
Nanus, Bert. *Visionary Leadership.*

On issues and trends, problems and opportunities in the world:
Myers, Bryant. *The New Context of World Missions.*
Johnstone, Patrick. *Operation World.*
Kennedy, Paul. *Preparing for the Twenty-First Century.*
Drucker, Peter. *Post-Capitalist Society.*
Subscribe to *National Geographic* and a newspaper or news magazine known for international coverage.

On strategizing and planning for missions involvement:
Engel, James. *Baby Boomers and the Future of World Missions.*
Mays, David. *Building Global Vision.*
Griffiths, Michael. *Get Your Church Involved in Missions.*
Camp, Bruce. *The Global Access Planner.*
ACMC. *Missions Policy Handbook.*
McGavran, Donald. *Momentous Decisions in Missions Today.*
Barrett, David. *Our Globe and How to Reach It.*

On preparing for cross-cultural ministry:
Elmer, Duane. *Cross-Cultural Conflict.*
Storti, Craig. *Cross-Cultural Dialogues.*
Bacon, Dan. *Equipping for Missions.*

Barnett, Betty. *Friend Raising.*
Lingenfelter, Sherwood. *Ministering Cross-Culturally.*
Dillon, Bill. *People Raising.*
Gration, John. *Steps to Getting Overseas.*
Griffiths, Michael. *Tinker, Tailor, Soldier, Missionary.*
Bacon, Dan. *What, Me a Missionary?*
Howard, David. *What Makes a Missionary.*

On short-term missions:
Anthony, Michael J., ed. *Short-Term Missions Boom.*
VanCise, Martha. *Successful Mission Teams.*
Aroney-Sine, Christine. *Survival of the Fittest.*
Eaton, Chris and Hurst, Kim. *Vacations with a Purpose*, leader's guide
and team member's manual.